P9-DMM-657

Consulting with Nonprofits
A Practitioner's Guide

Consulting with Nonprofits
A Practitioner's Guide

by Carol A. Lukas

We thank The David and Lucile Packard Foundation and the Amherst H. Wilder Foundation for underwriting the research and writing of this book.

Amherst H. Wilder Foundation
Saint Paul, Minnesota

This book was developed by Services to Organizations, a program of the Amherst H. Wilder Foundation in Saint Paul, Minnesota. Services to Organizations works in the Saint Paul-Minneapolis metropolitan area to strengthen the capacity of individuals, organizations, and other groups to improve their communities.

The Amherst H. Wilder Foundation is one of the largest and oldest endowed human service and community development organizations in America. For more than ninety years, the Wilder Foundation has been providing health and human services that help children and families grow strong, the elderly age with dignity, and the community grow in its ability to meet its own needs.

We hope you find this book helpful! Should you need additional information about our services, please contact: Services to Organizations, Amherst H. Wilder Foundation, 919 Lafond Avenue, Saint Paul, MN 55104, phone (612) 642-4022.

For information about other Wilder Foundation publications, please see the order form at the back of this book or contact: Publishing Center, Amherst H. Wilder Foundation, 919 Lafond Avenue, Saint Paul, MN 55104, 1-800-274-6024.

Edited by Vince Hyman
Illustrated by John Berry
Designed by Rebecca Andrews

Manufactured in the United States of America

First printing, July 1998

Library of Congress Cataloging-in-Publication Data

Lukas, Carol Ann
     Consulting with nonprofits : a practitioner's guide / by Carol Ann Lukas.
     p.   cm.
     Includes bibliographical references and index.
     ISBN 0-940069-17-2 (paperback)
     1. Consultants.   2. Community development consultants.   3. Nonprofit organizations--Management.
     I. Title.

HD69.C6L85 1998   98-21983
001'.068--dc21   CIP

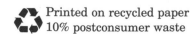

Printed on recycled paper
10% postconsumer waste

Acknowledgments

It took a community to write this book. I put the pen to paper, but many of the experiences and lessons belong to others. Many people provided support and encouragement during the writing. Thank you . . .

The David and Lucile Packard Foundation provided funding and are strong advocates for capacity building in the nonprofit sector. Barbara Kibbe encouraged and guided me and facilitated reviews by Bay Area consultants.

The Wilder Publishing Center, Vince Hyman, Becky Andrews, and Kirsten Lukens, are tremendously patient and skilled miracle workers with authors and publications. Vince gently and firmly hounded me, motivated me, and helped me organize my thinking. Cynthia MacLeod did great research on resources.

Many consultants across the country reviewed the manuscript and contributed rich stories from their combined four hundred plus years of experience. You gave the book life: Mike Allison, Emil Angelica, Carol Barbeito, Bryan Barry, Diane Brown, Paul Connolly, Barbara Davis, Terry Donovan, Michael Garcia, Michael Groh, Larry Guillot, William Hall, Grace Hammond, Bette Huntalas, Jill Janov, Robert Kardon, Rolfe Larson, David Martin, Pixie Martin, John B. McHugh, Carter McNamara, Kathryn Merchant, Patty Oertel, Matt O'Grady, Greg Owen, Vijit Ramchandani, Karen Simmons, Somly Sitthisay, Sally Smith, Gary J. Stern, Jim Thomas, Jeanne Toms, Patti Tototzintle, Robert Walker, and Ruth Yellow Hawk.

My colleagues in Services to Organizations and Communities at Amherst H. Wilder Foundation, as well as the many consultants and organizations in the community I've worked with over the years, continue to teach and challenge me.

A major source for the material is from my reading of countless books and professional articles over the years. An early consulting mentor once told me that the best way to get good and stay good as a consultant was to read at least a half hour every day. Just keep reading, he told me. I've tried to honor that advice. After many years and the hundreds of consulting projects I've done, I may have confused what I've learned from other authors and what I've learned from practice. I've tried to reference, at least generally, work from other sources. If I've not referenced someone's work appropriately I beg forgiveness.

My support system backed me up, covered for me, fed me, and made me laugh: Emil Angelica, Michael Gause, Kate Murphy, Barb Rose, Kay Tellekson, and Carol Zapfel. Brenna Barrett and Christopher Barrett hung through it all with me down to the finish line.

Carol Lukas
July 1998

About the Author

Carol Lukas, Program Manager and Senior Consultant with the Amherst
H. Wilder Foundation, has over twenty-five years consulting and training
experience with neighborhood, community development, health care,
education, environment, arts, and human service organizations, as well as
government agencies, foundations, collaborations, small businesses, and
major corporations. Carol focuses on building connections between the
public, private, and nonprofit sectors, and working with citywide and
regional coalitions to revitalize the central neighborhoods of Saint Paul.
She specializes in helping organizations and collaboratives plan and
manage change in services, organizational structure, dynamics, and
systems, and assists with strategic planning, community planning, coalitions and mergers, organizational assessment, restructuring, governance,
and conflict management. She also manages Wilder Foundation's community forums and publication of *Community Matters* and is former director
of Wilder Foundation's consulting and training services.

Contents

Preface

The job of running a nonprofit organization or successfully managing a community- or neighborhood-based agency is becoming increasingly complex and competitive. Strapped for resources and buffeted by economic and political forces while trying to address growing needs in the community, these organizations face enormous challenges, as well as opportunities. Many have the resources to hire consultants, planners, trainers, technical advisers, researchers, and facilitators to assist them in this enormous task; many do not.

This book is written for the growing numbers of consultants who provide various kinds of help to nonprofit and community organizations. It's also written as a guide for those who haven't yet started consulting but who, after retirement, education, or job changes, may begin. But behind those people are the thousands of nonprofit and community organizations who need highly skilled practitioners to assist them in addressing the formidable needs in our communities. The real goal of the book is to strengthen the quality of consulting available to these organizations to help them do the work of meeting human needs, educating and enriching our society, and building stronger, vital communities.

More than thirty consultants from across the country contributed ideas and stories and challenged my thinking during the development of this book. The final book is immeasurably enhanced by the participation of these people. Collectively, these contributors have over four hundred years of nonprofit consulting experience.

This book can be used in several ways:

- Those who have chosen the field of nonprofit consulting as a profession will find the book useful as a reference or a way to organize what they are already doing, whether they learned it through professional training or experience.

- People with technical specialties such as performing arts, accounting, education, social work, or housing will find the book provides a perspective on organizational and process issues encountered while consulting.

- Those who are new to the field of consulting may use the book as orientation to the field and a step-by-step guide through a particular consulting project.

- Consultants in the for-profit or public sectors can use the book to develop the skills and sensitivities needed when working with nonprofits.

- Funders can learn more about what to look for when funding consultation or technical assistance to their grantees.

- Students in public administration, nonprofit management, organization development, or related fields may find it a useful guide for fieldwork, service projects, or future career search.

The book is divided into five sections:

Chapter One	The Environment: Consultation and the Nonprofit Sector
Chapter Two	The Process: Stages of the Consulting Process
Chapter Three	Artistry: Consulting Roles, Dynamics, and Ethics
Chapter Four	Nuts and Bolts: Managing Your Consulting Practice
Appendices	Resources and Tools: Further Readings And Sources, Worksheets

CHAPTER ONE

The Environment

Consultation and the Nonprofit Sector

When I started consulting in the early 1970s, few nonprofits knew what a consultant did, and there were few of us around. In the last twenty-five years the field has exploded. Most large cities have organizations that manage groups of consultants or broker consulting services to nonprofits. Many funders and United Ways regularly support the cost of consultation to nonprofits. Consultation has become part of doing business in the nonprofit sector.

This chapter is intended to orient the reader to the field of consultation in the nonprofit sector. It will provide basic information on the nonprofit sector and the current environment; define consulting and explore the most common kinds of consulting provided to nonprofit and community groups; and orient the reader to some unique elements of consulting with nonprofits.

The Need for Consultants in the Nonprofit Sector

There are an estimated 1.4 million nonprofit organizations in the United States, with operating expenditures of approximately $500 billion as of 1993. Combined, these organizations represent approximately 6.5 percent of the U.S. gross national product and exceed the gross national products of all but a dozen countries worldwide[1]. Most organizations working in the arts, education, health care, human services, environment, community development, faith-based, and civic arenas are nonprofit. In addition, countless unincorporated community groups and neighborhood and civic associations emerge to address community needs or the interests of their members.

Nonprofit organizations are tax-exempt, nongovernmental, self-governing organizations that, unlike for-profit corporations, do not distribute profits to their directors and do exist to serve a public purpose. The destinies of these organizations rise and fall with economic fluctuations, changes in federal and state administrations and policies, private funding trends, and their own ability to generate revenues. The environment is dynamic and challenging.

Nonprofit organizations and community groups (referring to unincorporated and informal groups, associations, and coalitions, some of which exist for long periods of time) are struggling to address increasingly complex social, cultural, environmental, and economic needs in the communities they serve. Poverty, violence, disengagement of youth, stresses on the family, changes in the welfare system, managed care, growing populations of immigrants and non-English-speaking people, the transformation of our industrial economy into a service and information-based economy, suburban migration, and environmental hazards, among other factors, are requiring innovative responses from the nonprofit sector, which historically has focused on social needs, cultural enrichment, community development, health care, and education.

Trying to do everything with tight resources has always been the prevailing mode for nonprofits. Competition for funding and customers is fierce, and those organizations with visionary leadership, strong networks, and solid management infrastructure tend to thrive. Collaboration, joint ventures, and alliances have become a primary strategy to extend impact on limited resources, but organizations struggle to lead those alliances and absorb the additional time and energy they require with already heavy workloads.

---

[1] Lester Salamon, *Holding the Center: America's Nonprofit Sector at a Crossroads*, New York: Nathan Cummings Foundation, http//www.ncf.org, 1997.

To effectively address these community needs in a turbulent environment, funders and nonprofits are looking for better evaluation of impact, greater accountability, and innovative, collaborative responses that test the mettle of even the strongest and most creative nonprofit organizations.

Responding to these trends is a challenge for any organization, whether a new, emerging grassroots group, a more stable organization that needs to adjust program focus or capacity, or a larger and older nonprofit that has well-established services and financial base. Few nonprofits have the management or technical specialists on staff to deal with the spectrum of development needed to run an organization. Most nonprofits and community groups occasionally, or regularly, turn to outside resources for information, counsel, expertise, support, or process assistance.

The good news is that the nonprofit infrastructure—those organizations that provide technical assistance and other resources to nonprofits—has grown rapidly over the last fifteen years. For the purposes of this book I will lump all of these resources that assist nonprofit organizations into one large category that I will call *consultants*. There is a big difference between the work of a researcher doing a neighborhood demographic study, a social worker designing an after-school program, a facilitator leading focus groups, an arts consultant advising a museum about accreditation standards, and a planner developing a strategic plan. But there are a lot of commonalities among them as well. Providing resources and tools that will help these people provide high-quality assistance to nonprofit and community groups is the goal of this book.

Definition of Consultation

Consultation is a temporary relationship to provide assistance to a person, group, organization, or community wanting to build their capacity, accomplish a task, or achieve a goal. The consulting relationship differs from an employee relationship in that it is time-limited and the consultant is free to determine how and when to work.

Two elements are key in this definition of consultation—the accomplishment of a goal or task, and the consulting relationship. Consultation involves the accomplishment of a goal or task. The consultant is hired to do something—facilitate a process, evaluate a program, or develop a plan. A consultant is chosen because the client[2] needs to accomplish a task or

---

[2] The use of the word *client* disturbs some people, but I haven't found an alternative word that isn't awkward. The concern is that the word *client* objectifies a person or group, or suggests that they are in some way needy or helpless. Some consultants use terminology such as *partner, customer, ally,* or *participant*. Throughout this book I will use the word *client* focusing on the respectful meaning of the word as a person or group who deserves our best attention and quality of service, and with whom we have formed a partnership to do some work.

goal, and the consultant has skills or expertise that will assist the client in accomplishing this work. As the consulting project is developed the second element becomes important. A relationship is formed, usually temporary, that contributes to success in accomplishing the task. Key aspects of a successful consultant-client relationship are trust and reciprocity. Trust is needed to allow the client to speak freely about the organizational situation or dynamics and to help the consultant feel free to challenge, probe, and explore alternative choices. Reciprocity is important to ensure that the power relationship is balanced and that two-way influence and effective communication will occur. A third element of consultation involves an exchange of value between the consultant and the client; work is done in exchange for pay, acknowledgment, or other benefits that may derive from the partnership.

The biggest problem I face as a consultant is if the chemistry is wrong with the client. It's the toughest part of consulting. It's almost an art form to establish and maintain good working relationships.

— *William P. Hall*
Volunteer Consultant, Executive Service Corps of Chicago

Consultation involves more than the transfer of information or advice. What is often not understood, either by consultants or by nonprofits and community groups, is that there is a body of knowledge and skills involved in the process of consulting that is different from, and in addition to, a person's technical or content expertise. In some ways consulting is like teaching. To be a teacher one has to know a body of information. But that knowledge alone doesn't make a good teacher. A good teacher has additional skills such as alternative ways of transferring knowledge, instilling a love of learning, adapting to different learning styles, motivating students, and speaking from the heart. Really good teachers know that there is an art to teaching, and concrete skills and sensitivities involved in the teaching process, regardless of what they are teaching. Chapter Two in this book will focus on the process of consulting, and Chapter Four will cover skills needed as a consultant.

A successful consultation with an organization or a group ends with at least two kinds of results:

1. *The client accomplishes their goals.*

   The organization or group successfully accomplishes the goals that they hired the consultant to help them with. This may include the accomplishment of a particular task, the creation of a product, acquisition of knowledge, or the strengthening of relationships within the organization. Occasionally the goals of a project change in midstream to respond to changing circumstances or new information. An effective consultation will adjust to these changes and work toward goals that serve the client's needs.

2. *The client increases their capacity to deal with similar issues in the future.*

The organization or group learns skills or processes to deal more effectively with future challenges as they emerge and to make appropriate decisions about seeking outside help when needed. Ideally, the organization or group learns how to maintain a healthy state of adaptability to changing conditions and to maximize the strengths and resources in the group for ongoing creative improvements. Working toward this result means that you, as the consultant, deliberately try to build the capacity of the client to minimize their need for your assistance on similar issues in the future.

In a sense, one of our goals as consultants is to eliminate the need for our services in the future—or to work ourselves out of a job. As we discussed, consulting is a temporary relationship. In reality I find that the more effectively I help the client accomplish the second goal, the more they come back to me for additional assistance. The difference is that usually they aren't coming back for the same help. Their capacity is increased, and they are taking on different or more innovative projects. This is not true when the consultant repeatedly does the same work and takes work direction from the organization. (With an ongoing relationship you may be a staff person on a contract rather than a consultant. For those of you working in the U.S., see Appendix E, The Difference between Employee and Independent Contractor, on page 213, for the Internal Revenue Service's distinction between an employee and independent contractor.)

The goals of the consulting relationship and the process of consulting are similar regardless of the kind of consulting we do. Let's look now at the rich diversity in kinds of consulting and the backgrounds of people providing consultation with nonprofits and community groups.

Kinds of Consultation

An amazing assortment of people in the community have *consultant* on their business card. Since there are no licensing bodies or certification required for someone to work as a consultant (except with certain professions such as accounting, fund-raising, or law), anyone with the moxie to call themselves a consultant and the luck to find a client can become a consultant. This is good and bad. The lack of professional standards and training requirements allows anyone to hang a shingle, whether they have skills or not. The lack of certification standards also makes it difficult for nonprofit organizations and community groups to select a skilled consultant other than on personal knowledge or referral source claims. On the other hand, in addition to professionally trained consultants, many people in the community, including experienced nonprofit directors and community leaders, technical specialists, business professionals, and retirees, have tremendous gifts to share. The lack of rigorous standards or certification makes it easy for these resources to be accessed by potential nonprofit clients.

Among those who have hung their shingle as consultants, three categories of consulting are most commonly provided to nonprofit organizations and community groups. These three categories, *program* consultation, *organizational* consultation, and *community* consultation, differ in skills required, who the client is, and scope of work.

1. Program Consultation

Program consultants are often specialists in a particular program area, such as child care, workforce development, home-based services for the elderly, or theater production. Program consultants might assist their clients with program design and planning, program assessment, staff development, or evaluation. For example: a *housing* consultant might have broad experience in developing various forms of low-income housing. An *elderly services* consultant may have expertise in different community-based approaches for serving the elderly. A *community health care* consultant might have experience bringing home health care to underserved populations, and bring "best-practice" ideas to a local clinic. Or a *dance* consultant might assist a dance company with developing a training program for new members of the company.

Clinical consultants, commonly used in psychiatric, mental health, education, or social work organizations, are often called in to assist the client with program recipients who pose challenging or new issues unfamiliar to the client. Such consultants may provide a diagnostic or advisory service, or train clinical staff to work with new or difficult issues emerging within the population served by the client. A school that has traditionally worked with native-born students might hire a consultant who understands the culture and unique needs of students from refugee communities.

People working as program consultants usually emerge from the trenches in their area of specialty. They are often staff of a nonprofit that offers direct service in that program area, and they provide consultation to other nonprofit organizations in the same line of work. For example, a nonprofit serving the Hmong community may offer a consulting service to other organizations who have growing numbers of Hmong clients. In fact, a typical earned-income strategy for nonprofit organizations is to start a consulting or training business in their area of expertise, assisting other organizations—in the same region or in other parts of the country—with program development or implementation. Program consultants also work independently, without affiliation with a nonprofit.

2. Organizational Consultation

In organizational consultation, the consultant is concerned with the functioning of all or part of an organization, usually with the aim of improving its effectiveness or viability. The consultant may focus on functional areas and systems (e.g., finance, human resources, facilities, marketing, fund development, information management, evaluation), culture (e.g., values, norms, environment, climate), leadership and structure (e.g., governance, management, structure, staffing), or dynamics (e.g., relationships, decision making, problem solving, communications). The consultant might work with individuals, groups, or the organization as a whole. Whatever the focus, the aim of organizational consultation is to enhance the effectiveness of the organization and the people who work there to accomplish its mission.

Generalist vs. Specialist

Organizational consultants can either be generalists or specialists. There is need for both approaches, but the advantages and limitations of each are important to know.

A specialist consultant usually has technical expertise in one or two functional areas. For instance, a *technology* consultant may have a thorough understanding of software and hardware, and how to plan for and set up systems, but might not know about overall organizational planning. Other examples of specialist consultants are *accountants, fund-raisers, researchers, financial planners, marketing consultants*, and *benefits/compensation* experts. Some planning consultants are specialists too—they are experts in directing the *process* of planning only without experience or expertise in the management of organizations. The client organization, in this case, ensures content quality of the plan and oversees the integration of plans.

The advantage of a specialist approach is that the client gets highly focused, in-depth expertise in a particular area. The limitation is that the specialist often isn't aware of the interrelationships between what they're working on and other functions in the organization or group. For example, a graphic designer may assist an organization in developing promotional materials. The quality of the promotional materials might be outstanding. But the consultant may have accepted the client's description of what the materials should say without questioning what the promotional goals of the organization are, whether the organization has the leadership and capacity to deliver on the increased business that the materials might produce, or whether the promotional strategy is appropriate given the mission, values, and goals of the organization.

As a specialist consultant in nonprofit publishing, a major problem I face is that publishing is one function within a bigger whole and often gets subsumed in the larger picture. So my clients face challenges in the larger organization such as fit with overall strategy, trying to get decisions made, and volunteer power trips. I need to help my clients figure out what they want to accomplish with their publishing and how that fits into the larger organization. In one instance a board wanted to manage the day-to-day publishing operations, and they weren't equipped to do that. They ended up trying to force bad publishing decisions on staff. Staff were intimidated by the board. We set up policies and procedures that institutionalized decision making about publishing. In another case I worked with a large organization that had rapidly grown their publishing business. They were successful, but disorganized. The structure didn't serve a publishing function, and they had amateurs where they needed experienced people. I raised concerns about the structure and was told not to fool with it—that was how they wanted it. I would change it dramatically if I was looking at it as a pure publishing function. But they were clear about what they wanted and didn't want. When consulting on one function within an organization, I try to understand and take into consideration the broader organizational situation. But sometimes I have to walk away because it's "mission impossible" for the consultant.

— *John B. McHugh*
McHugh Publishing and Consulting

Generalists have a broad knowledge of a range of functions within an organization and are able to see the interrelationship between functions. Generalists are often hired when there are a variety of concerns with how an organization is functioning, or when the organization wants to grow or change in a particular direction. Consultants who do *planning* are often generalists, because they often help the organization develop overall strategies for program, personnel, facilities, or finance—functions that can directly affect one another. Planning consultants usually know enough about a range of functions to integrate different issues in an organizational plan.

The advantage of generalists is that they *do* see interrelationships among the functions of an organization and often provide a big-picture view of how changes affect the different parts of the organization. Their limitation: generalists may not have enough in-depth knowledge of an area to know when they're missing something. Ideally they will know enough to determine when to bring in someone else to supplement their work—someone with a specialist set of skills. For example, a strategic planning consultant may assist the client in looking broadly at the organization's history, mission, strengths, capabilities, and strategic opportunities, and develop a plan with the client to move the organization into the future. But in taking the broad view and relying on the assessment of organizational members, they may miss some issues that are crucial to the organization's future success, such as leadership skills, financial condition, or program quality.

There is wonderful variety in the types of organizational consulting done and the skills and expertise that consultants bring to their work. It's important for both the consultant and the client to clarify together what kind of consulting is needed and desired and whether the potential consultant is experienced in providing that consulting assistance.

Organization Development

Organization development (OD) is a particular kind of organizational consulting in which behavior science principles are applied to individual, group, and organizational dynamics for long-term, system-wide planned change. Emerging in the late 1950s and early 1960s, the OD field over the years has spawned a variety of "movements"—quality improvement, sociotechnical systems, open systems planning, organization effectiveness, organization transformation, and learning organizations, among others. The discipline of organization development is often misrepresented as "organizational development," which usually means the process of starting an organization.

Over the last fifteen years, the nonprofit sector has increasingly used OD consultants, usually for more limited or specialty interventions such as leadership development, diversity training, conflict resolution, or team-building. These interventions are specialties within the field of organization development. A one- or two-day leadership development workshop, or a day-long team-building session is not necessarily focused on system-wide, long-term planned change. The argument for short-term OD interventions is that if the organization is having problems and they only have four hours to invest, why not do what you can? Perhaps the short-term work will lead to continued change over the long term. The OD purist might counter that giving the organization a Band-Aid intervention may mask more systemic issues that will only get worse over time.

Specialist interventions, however, are the type of OD consulting that nonprofits most often request. The majority of nonprofit organizations are small and have limited resources. They don't have the time, energy, or money to engage in longer-term, more systemic change processes. They want to focus on the nuts and bolts of improving functions or solving a problem in the here and now.

Organizational consultants enter the field by a variety of routes:

- *Executive directors*: Some consultants begin in a nonprofit organization at the program level and gain expertise in that program field. They then move up in the organization through management roles and eventually become an executive director. After years as an executive director, the person may opt for a career change and decide to become a consultant to other nonprofit organizations and groups.

- *For-profit consultants*: Some consultants in the for-profit sector make the switch to the nonprofit sector, or supplement their for-profit consulting. They may have heard the nonprofit sector holds opportunities, or they may want a change of focus in their career.

- *Program specialists*: Some consultants have experience as a teacher, psychologist, or therapist with skills in individual, group, and intergroup interventions that are transferable to organizational consulting.

- *For-profit managers and technical specialists*: Some consultants leave jobs in management or functional specialist roles (e.g., an attorney or technology expert) and start consulting with nonprofits in those areas.

- *Retired, pre-retired or loaned executives*: More and more corporations are downsizing their staffs, creating a massive baby-boomer pre-retirement pool of executives with management expertise. Even if they aren't downsizing, corporations may give time off to their executives to volunteer with nonprofits, an acknowledgment of their community responsibility. Some communities and United Ways have set up technical assistance brokering services that loan expertise from the for-profit sector to nonprofits. Groups like the National Executive Service Corps and SCORE have been set up to use the expertise of retired executives in helping nonprofits.

- *Students and faculty*: Colleges and universities are increasingly providing degree programs in nonprofit management and organizational studies, public administration, and public policy. Students and faculty in these programs often work as consultants with nonprofits.

- *Organization development generalists*: Consultants practicing OD usually have graduate-level training in organization development, organization behavior, industrial psychology, or a related field.

Many consultants working in the nonprofit sector are independent practitioners working in a sole proprietorship. Some consultants have started a small agency or an informal or legal partnership with other consultants. Some independent consultants also have a full-time or part-time job and do their consulting as a sideline.

In many of the larger cities across the country, management support organizations (MSOs) exist that either hire consultants on a staff basis or broker volunteers as consultants to nonprofits. MSOs can be freestanding or might be attached to a United Way, foundation, or university. Most MSOs offer a variety of organizational consulting and technical assistance.

I kind of slid into consulting work. I was employed by a large organization and had no idea what a consultant was, although I had worked with some freelance people like graphic designers and editors. We had tremendous turmoil in our department and they called in a consultant who did a series of interviews to try to understand what was going on. His contract was cut short and my supervisors didn't implement any of the changes we worked on with him despite the great job I thought he did. I had never experienced someone working independently before. I had no models for what a consultant did, or how someone became a consultant. I called and interviewed him, and we ended up working on a project together. He started his consulting work on a path similar to mine. He had severed ties with a large organization. He started looking for a job but found he wasn't finding the kind of work he wanted to do. He started telling people what he was able to do. Then he started helping people with things on a volunteer basis. He found that he was more satisfied, doing work he loved, and on top of that he found he could earn more money than he would've at a "job." Eventually he called himself a consultant.

— *Pixie Martin*
Independent Consultant

3. Community Consultation

Community consultation differs from program and organizational consultation in scope of work, definition of the client, and complexity of "political" issues involved. Community consultation differs from consulting in an organizational setting in several significant ways:

- *Scope of work*: In community consultation, the consultant often deals with many different organizations, associations, political interests, and citizen groups. Because of this, the range of issues being dealt with may be broad. The focus of the consulting work might include, simultaneously, housing, public health, school programming, crime prevention, business creation, and mental health. Implementation roles may be assigned to dozens of different organizations and groups. The final plan or chosen decision may need approval from many participating agencies and several layers of city government, as well as the city council and neighborhood associations. The scope of work is broader than program or organizational consulting, the issues are more complex, and additional and more flexible skills are needed.

- *Who the client is*: In community consultation, the client is often a collaborative among various entities in a geographic area, or among organizations that share similar missions in different geographic areas. The client may be an organization that has taken leadership of the project, or representatives of several community-based organizations and groups who are collaborating on a project. The client may be an informal alliance of people who have come together in a neighborhood to get something done. Or the client may be a large system such as a state- or citywide network. Unless there is a formal association with defined roles, responsibility for directing a consultant is often ad hoc rather than institutionally defined as it is in an organization.

- *Who is at the table*: Consulting with community groups, collaboratives, or grassroots organizations often means dealing with a wide variety of people, special interests, and values. People sitting at the same decision-making table might include all or any combination of the following: individual citizens, business owners, elected officials, neighborhood activists, school representatives, community-based organizations, different ethnic or cultural groups, foundations, institutions, city government staff, neighborhood associations, and advocacy or special interest groups. Inclusion is important. Finding and sustaining common focus among such diverse interests is a unique challenge; I liken it to herding cats. In addition, many community meetings are public, and some attract the media. At one meeting you expect twenty people and get sixty; at another you expect seventy-five and get eight.

- *How decisions are made*: Shared power, locally owned solutions, and consensus decision making are terms and practices common in community consultation. There is often a strong value for and practice of one voice, one vote. An individual's position in their "home" organization (for example, executive director) doesn't necessarily give them more power than an individual citizen in making decisions. At a minimum, without the predefined hierarchy of an organizational structure, deciding how to make decisions becomes a crucial early step in a consulting project. The lines of decision making are seldom as clear as in other kinds of consulting. Usually many people need to be part of decisions to get ownership and buy-in from various constituencies.

Community consultants come from a wide variety of places. Some, like neighborhood planning consultants, come from professional roles in community organizations, government, or academia. Others move into consulting roles after years in the trenches doing community work. Still others move into community consultation from their work as organizational or program consultants.

Orientation to Nonprofit Consulting

I am clearly biased toward consulting in the nonprofit sector. I find the leadership and management of nonprofit organizations challenging, the people working in nonprofits principled, passionate, and committed, and organizational missions compelling. I can argue with vigor the travesty of reducing national support for arts organizations; the pros and cons of managed care and the impact it's having on the quality of health care in this country; the irreparable damage uncontrolled suburban sprawl is causing in our inner cities; and the vital importance of making recipients of human services participants in providing their own care—all critical concerns of many nonprofits. I am fascinated by the infinite varieties of nonprofit boards, and delight in exploring new ways for a community-based nonprofit to connect better with their constituencies. I form strong connections with nearly every organization and group with which I work. That has not always been the case in my consulting work within the for-profit sector. Nonprofit work represents, for me, deeply rooted values and beliefs. When I work with nonprofit organizations and community issues, my values and work are aligned. Therein, for me, is the joy. But that is my story.

In many ways consultation is the same regardless of the kind of organization or group with which you are working. The consultant's goal—**to assist a person, group, organization, or community to build their capacity, accomplish a task, or achieve a goal**—is the same. The steps in the process are similar, the relationship issues are always paramount, and the work itself can be almost identical. The consultant has to enter into the system, learn about the client's goals, work, systems, culture, and people, and provide assistance so that the client accomplishes their goals and increases their capacity to deal with similar issues in the future.

In other ways, nonprofit consulting is different from consulting with for-profit and public organizations. In addition to differences in bottom line, ownership, tax structure, funding, and reporting, there are differences in language, culture, and norms. In addition, many consultants choose to work in the nonprofit sector because of the importance and intrinsic meaning of the work done by nonprofits. The opportunity to work for the benefit of society, whether in the arts, environment, education, human services, or community development, and earn a living doing it is a privilege. For many people this is dramatically different from consulting in the for-profit sector, which carries its own unique rewards and challenges.

It is difficult to generalize about nonprofit organizations. There is a huge variety in missions, types, sizes, styles, and cultures of nonprofit organizations. Organizational cultures and types of business vary widely, and organizational size and age differences produce different developmental challenges. There are far more consulting similarities between a food shelf with an annual budget of $150,000 and a small family-owned business than there are between the food shelf and a national foundation that is also a nonprofit. Age of the organization and the extent to which procedures and norms are institutionalized are other key variables. A fledgling nonprofit with an entrepreneurial spirit can be similar to an emerging for-profit venture, and different from an established century-old nonprofit.

Throughout the text I refer to nonprofit organizations and community groups. For the purposes of this book I am including organizations incorporated as nonprofit corporations, and informal, unincorporated associations, groups, and coalitions. The Internal Revenue Service (IRS) has more than twenty different classifications for nonprofit organizations. The largest classification is charitable corporations (501(c)(3), followed by civic leagues and local associations (501(c)(4) and fraternal associations (501(c)(8)[3]. In addition countless unincorporated associations, coalitions, and community-based groups exist to provide a service or product to their constituents. An increasing amount of work in the nonprofit sector is being done through coalitions and collaborations between multiple organizations. I am not including consulting with the public sector (government), although a lot of the book describes processes that can apply to government groups. Government agencies have some unique characteristics that make consultation with them different from consultation with nonprofit organizations.

Most nonprofits are created to bring a benefit to society and its members or to respond to an unmet need in the community. Nonprofit corporations are usually started by a few dedicated individuals with a mission—to create a forum for emerging writers, to advocate for harsher drug possession laws, to start a community clinic, to begin a charter school, or to support more aggressive research into treatment of brain injuries. The steps for starting a nonprofit vary by state, but in general include: selecting a name; writing and filing articles of incorporation with the Secretary of State; writing bylaws; and obtaining tax-exempt status from the IRS. With that the nonprofit is in business.

Nonprofit organizations have boards of directors that govern the affairs of the corporation. Boards are entrusted with the leadership and governance of the nonprofit. Nonprofit board members do not receive personal gain from the actions of the corporation, unlike for-profit directors; they serve in a volunteer capacity. Boards can vary from three to fifty or more in size. The precise structure and role of the board is spelled out in the organization's bylaws. Some boards operate as a team of volunteers who

---

[3] Roger A. Lohmann, *The Commons*, from the Jossey-Bass Nonprofit Sector Series (San Francisco: Jossey-Bass, 1992).

staff the organization; others serve a policy-setting or advisory role and are not involved in the day-to-day affairs of the organization. Most boards who are successful at raising funds eventually hire staff to do the work of the organization. The internal structure varies by organization but usually includes an executive director, administrative staff, and program staff. In larger nonprofits the organizational structure can be similar to that of for-profit corporations.

Nonprofits include a statement of purpose in their articles of incorporation. This purpose is usually referred to as their mission and provides their reason for existence and a guide for programming and operating decisions. For nonprofits, their mission is their bottom line. Their success as an organization is gauged by their progress at achieving their mission. Nonprofits usually engage in a variety of work that helps them achieve this mission. The job of the board of directors is to ensure that a fair swap occurs between the contributions of donors, customers, and funders, and the benefits or outcomes produced.

Nonprofit organizations, when tax-exempt, are able to receive tax-deductible contributions and grants to finance their operations. Increasingly nonprofits are pursuing earned-income strategies, including fees for service, sale of products, and rental of facilities to reduce their dependence on grants. However, many still rely on individual donations, grants, and government contracts for the majority of their income. Payment for services often comes from a third party rather than directly from the recipient of service. Because of the sometimes fierce competition for funding, nonprofits are often lean operations. Hiring a consultant is usually a big deal, market rate consultant fees often shock them, and they tolerate few extra "bells and whistles." They want the work done quickly and efficiently, with an eye on the price tag and an expectation of return on their investment.

Consultants who haven't experienced the nonprofit environment might want to educate themselves before embarking on a consulting project. It's difficult to generalize about how nonprofits operate, the nature of their business, and the organizational cultures. Nonprofits are as varied as for-profits. Some are large, others small. Some have rigid hierarchies; others are informal and collegial. Some have weak management; others are paragons of excellence in management. Some are diverse; others are homogeneous. Some are entrepreneurial; others conservative. Some are well endowed or have sophisticated and lucrative revenue streams; others scrape by, barely meeting payroll every week.

Many nonprofits have had bad experiences with for-profit consultants who want to expand their market and do work in the nonprofit sector. The problem is philosophy and language differences. The bottom line in the nonprofit sector is to change lives, not make money. For-profit consultants need to find a way to understand the nonprofit culture and see the diversity in the nonprofit sector—by reading, listening, whatever works with their learning style. One of the best ways is to experience being on a nonprofit board, even a couple of boards with organizations of different sizes. They can also link up with nonprofit peers, hook up with a management support organization, or do some volunteering as a consultant or trainer.

— *Diane Brown*
Non-Profit Assistance Group

Consultants whose experience is in the for-profit sector are surprised by three things when they start working with nonprofits. First, nonprofits are short on resources—people, money, and time. As a result, consulting projects take much longer than they anticipate. Second, because of the shortage of resources, there's a huge need for consulting help, and nonprofits ask for all kinds of extra help. It can be a real challenge to stick to the scope of the contract. Third, many for-profit consultants think that because a nonprofit is small they don't have the same problems as a for-profit. Nonprofits have the same challenges as for-profits, but because many of them are so small, they are dynamic. Change occurs rapidly and has greater impact than in a larger organization. Consulting contracts become obsolete quickly. A consultant will budget fifty hours to do strategic planning, find the board isn't engaged, and realize board development is needed before strategic planning. The consultant needs to be patient and help the client find a step-by-step process to work through their issues. And the consultant has to be willing to change the contract when the work changes.

— *Carter McNamara*
Independent Consultant, formerly with MAP for Nonprofits, which matches volunteers from the for-profit sector with nonprofits needing consulting assistance

At the risk of generalizing inappropriately about the nonprofit sector, the following characteristics will be true in most nonprofits:

- Management of a nonprofit requires the same attention to quality, production, sales, marketing, finance, human resources, facilities, and customers that management of a for-profit requires. There are differences that need to be understood by a consultant because of different tax laws and funding and financing strategies.

- Most people work in the nonprofit sector because they want to. Many boards and staff have deep commitment to their work and to their organizations. Commitment based on values is powerful and pervasive.

- Volunteers are commonly used in nonprofits either in place of staff or to extend the capacity of staff. Volunteer recruitment and management can be important in a nonprofit.

- Decision making often involves a lot of people, many of whom are board, staff, volunteers, constituents, residents, customers, and community members. Because of this it can take longer and be difficult as the various values and perspectives are considered. The payoff is that there can be great buy-in and support for decisions. It is important for consultants to know how to manage large-group decision-making processes.

- Nonprofits often provide services to, or have present on their staff and boards, representatives of diverse cultural communities and economic classes. Issues of equity, inclusion, accessibility, language, and style are regularly explored and dealt with. Consultants who don't have experience working across cultures or haven't experienced the nonprofit environment might consider finding a mentor or partnering with a consultant who is experienced in this environment.

- Many nonprofits operate on a lean budget. For-profit corporations can also operate on a lean budget, but the nonprofit definition of *lean* means really lean. Salaries tend to be lower in nonprofits than in the for-profit sector. Market consulting rates are difficult for many nonprofits to believe, much less pay. Nonprofits will often push a consultant to do things quickly and efficiently, and at reasonable cost.

I have learned how much orientation volunteers from the for-profit sector need before they can consult effectively in the nonprofit sector. In one situation, we had matched a volunteer consultant with a neighborhood organization to do strategic planning. The consultant called us the second week into the project, wanting to back out. He judged that because the executive didn't return phone calls and meetings were always being rescheduled, the client wasn't taking ownership of the problem; they weren't meeting the consultant halfway. We talked to the executive director and there were legitimate reasons: staff had been sick, the board chair moved, and the consultant was recommending resources and a time line that just weren't realistic given the budget. The volunteer consultant ended up staying with the project, and we coached him through the work. We later got a letter from the executive saying what a wonderful job the consultant had done. Based on this and similar experiences, we have started using a "buddy system" with consultants new to the nonprofit sector, pairing them with an experienced consultant.

— Carter McNamara
Independent Consultant, formerly with MAP for Nonprofits, which matches volunteers from the for-profit sector with nonprofits needing consulting assistance

The nonprofit sector provides a rich arena for the practice of consultation. The need is great and the work stimulating. Because of the unique characteristics of the nonprofit environment, consulting with nonprofits can be challenging, and extremely rewarding.

Chapter One Summary

In this chapter we explored the field of consultation in the nonprofit sector. We covered four topics:

- The need for consultants in the nonprofit sector
- Definition of consultation
- Kinds of consultation
- Orientation to nonprofit consulting

The remaining chapters in the book will explore the spirit, roles, and process of consulting in depth. To begin, Chapter Two outlines the stages of the consulting process. It will take you step-by-step through a consulting project from initial meeting to termination.

CHAPTER TWO

The Process

Stages of Consulting

As we discussed earlier, consulting is both a process and a relationship.

In this chapter we will focus on the process aspects of consulting—the systematic steps that lead from the first telephone call or inquiry for assistance to the accomplishment of the goals, delivery of the final "product," and termination of the relationship.

There are six stages in the consulting process[4]. Each of these stages involves specific tasks and choices for the consultant, and each has challenges to be maneuvered. The six stages of the consulting process, summarized below, will be described in depth, step-by-step, in this chapter.

---

[4] Many writers on consultation have described a similar consulting process, including Lippitt, Ronald, Jeanne Watson and Bruce Westley, *The Dynamics of Planned Change* (New York: Harcourt, Brace, 1958) and Lippitt, Gordon and Ronald Lippitt, *The Consulting Process in Action* (San Francisco: Jossey-Bass, 1986, pages 11-35).

The six stages of the consulting process are:

(pages 22–36)

Stage 1: Contracting

In the first stage you get a call from, meet, or introduce yourself to a potential client. You determine whether the kind of help they need or want fits with your capabilities, interests, style, and availability. You meet with them to explore a possible relationship and the scope of the work that might be involved. You reach agreement about whether and how to proceed into a consulting relationship. You formalize your relationship through a consulting contract or agreement, usually in writing.

(pages 37–63)

Stage 2: Gathering and Analyzing Data

The purpose of the second stage is to understand fully what the client is hoping to accomplish and what will be needed for them to achieve that. This often involves collecting and analyzing information that will help them, and you, make decisions about future actions. This step is sometimes done before the contracting in the first phase; more often it is done after you and the client have reached agreement on the consulting contract.

(pages 64–85)

Stage 3: Planning the Work

The third stage of the consulting process involves helping the client process the information that has been collected and clarify or define goals for change. You assist the client in developing goals, strategies, and a plan of action to bring about the desired change.

(pages 85–94)

Stage 4: Implementing and Monitoring

In the fourth stage of the consulting process you and the client implement the plans that were created in Stage 3. You monitor the implementation over time to ensure that events or changes have the intended effect and goals are accomplished. You make adjustments as needed to keep the project successful.

(pages 94–98)

Stage 5: Sustaining Change and Evaluating Impact

The purpose of the fifth stage is to determine the extent to which the activities involved in the consulting effort have the intended impact and are likely to continue into the future. You put mechanisms in place to ensure that the organization can continue progress in the future. You gather information and determine if goals have been achieved, or whether additional effort is needed on your or the client's part.

(pages 99–103)

Stage 6: Terminating the Consulting Project

Termination involves the formal, deliberate ending of the consulting relationship. You have finished the work that has been agreed upon, and all terms of the consulting contract have been met, or there is formal agreement to end the consulting relationship without completing the work.

These six stages are guideposts to help you and the client move through a consulting project. In real life they take different form in each consulting project you work on. I use them as a guide to planning my work, estimating time, and developing a proposal, and as a diagnostic tool for myself to assess how the consulting project is proceeding. When I get in difficulty on a project, it is usually because my work in one of the previous stages was incomplete, or because conditions or expectations changed and I need to move back a stage or two. Frequently the scope of work changes in the middle of the project and I need to go back to Stage 1: Contracting to clarify expectations with the client on how the changes in scope of work affect our agreement, work plan, and budget.

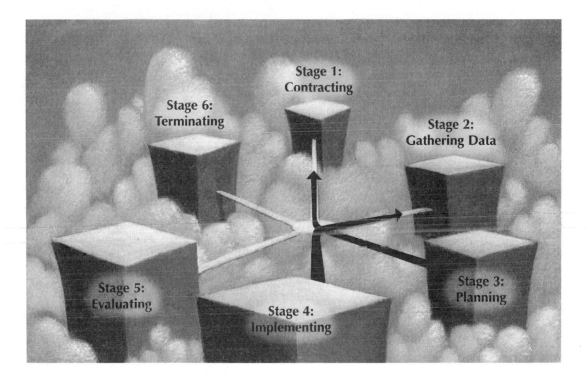

As the diagram above indicates, the stages are dynamic in practice. You may be working simultaneously in several of the stages at any given time in a consulting project. If you are helping the client develop strategies for the future, you may, at the same time, be recontracting to do an additional piece of data collection, and intervening with two members of the group who are in a conflict situation.

You will notice that there is significantly more emphasis in this chapter on Stages 1–3 than there is on Stages 4–6. In my experience, whenever I get in trouble in a consulting project it is due to problems in Stages 1–3. When these stages are done well, I sail through Stages 4–6.

The remainder of this chapter will explore the six stages in the consulting process in detail.

STAGE 1: Contracting

Contracting is the most pivotal stage of the consulting process. The goals are to decide whether there is a fit between your capabilities and the client's needs, to form a relationship with the client, and to reach agreement on the nature and scope of work to be done. How you execute the contracting stage will determine how well the consulting project will succeed. Problems occurring in later stages can often be tracked back to confusion, different expectations about, or incomplete work done in the contracting stage.

With some projects, this stage is completed in a ten-minute phone conversation and you sail through the project with ease. In other projects you can struggle to get agreement on the project for many months. In either case, the initial encounters between you and the client are important for both of you to decide whether to proceed into a consulting relationship.

The "fit" between you and the client involves more than just the work to be done. When asked why they chose one consultant over another, clients will often talk about the consultant's manner, style, sense of humor, political savvy, or various intangible characteristics. Other factors that can be important include experience with certain kinds of organizations, referrals from past clients, age, experience, race, gender, political affiliation, sensitivity to particular issues in the client system, or style in working with groups.

There are five steps in the contracting stage. These five steps will help you discover all the information you need to arrive at a good contract and form a constructive relationship with your client. These steps can be accomplished quickly or over time. They can be worked through over coffee or in formal boardrooms. They can be used with one person or with a large group. They are rarely sequential—you begin developing the consulting relationship during the first minute of your first conversation. They can result in a handshake agreement, a lengthy formal proposal, or a decision not to work together.

The following five steps in the contracting stage of the consulting process will be described in detail:

1. Understand the organization and the work to be done

2. Describe your background and experience as a consultant

3. Begin developing the consulting relationship

4. Develop a proposal or written agreement

5. Decide whether to proceed with a consulting relationship

Step 1: Understand the Organization and the Work to Be Done

You will have many questions about the client, their organization, neighborhood, or group, and about the work that they would like you to do. I usually start by exploring the work the client wants done. When I understand that, and feel that the work is in sync with my capabilities and interests, I proceed to learn more about the organization or group. My discussion with a potential client includes the following:

- *Clarify objectives of the consulting project:* What is the client hoping to accomplish? In some cases the outcome is concrete and easy to describe—a strategic plan, evaluation of a program, or a decision about purchasing a building. In other cases the outcome is harder to define—improved morale, or better relationships among board members. In either case it is important for the client to define how they will know when that outcome has been reached so that both the client and the consultant are working toward the same result and have a way of measuring when the work has been completed successfully.

- *Gain an understanding of the organization or community group:* What is their mission and history? What work do they do? Who are their audiences and constituencies? How does this project relate to their core programs and services? Who are the key decision makers? What values drive the organization? Who is on the board and staff? How do they make decisions?

I've learned to spend time in advance of an initial meeting to get to know the group I'm going to work with. I'm confident in my expertise; the challenge for me is in listening and learning who the client is, what their style is, and working within their framework. In one case a nonprofit health care facility in a rural area asked me to recommend some new financial management policies. Luckily I asked some questions before I first met with them. I got to know a little about their culture. I had to get used to the cadence of their speech. I'm from an urban area and needed to adapt my speech and dress. (The director later told me that if I had worn a suit to the first meeting I would've made them uncomfortable.) The project went well, and in the end, the board approved all of my recommendations.

— *Rolfe Larson*
Rolfe Larson Associates

- *Clarify the opportunity, problem, or need that the group wants to address:* Often your assessment of what the client needs will be different than the client's "presenting problem." Does the client's definition of the opportunity or problem or their idea about what needs to be done seem to be the real issue that needs to be addressed? You and the client will need to explore whether other factors in the situation are critical enough to warrant a change in the nature or scope of consulting work from the client's initial concept. Examples of this might include:

  A client asks you to develop a brochure for a new project. When you start exploring how this brochure will be used and what they hope to accomplish, you find that the client isn't clear about the target audience and what features that audience would find valuable about the new project. You may conclude that the client needs to do some market research and develop a marketing plan before they invest in promotional material.

  Or:

  You are asked to facilitate a strategic planning retreat for the board of a neighborhood association. In your discussion with the community organizer who contacted you, you discover that there is a major conflict simmering on the board about whether the organizer's public statements on a controversial issue were in violation of organizational policy. You may conclude that the conflict needs to be resolved before the board begins its annual planning process.

- *Assess the likelihood of success:* Are any factors present that might hinder success in this project or undertaking? Consider leadership, past history with similar efforts, willingness to commit the necessary time and resources, and readiness for change or new ideas. Will the work you are being asked to do be likely to have the impact the client anticipates? Are there realistic expectations?

Step 2: Describe Your Background and Experience as a Consultant

The consulting relationship is an exchange relationship. You do work for a client. They select you because you have a particular set of skills, knowledge, or abilities that they need to accomplish a particular goal. In exchange for your assistance, you receive something of value. Often it is a fee for the work done. Sometimes the work is done pro bono—without a fee. Even with pro bono work, the consultant receives something. The value received can be experience with consulting; exposure to a certain kind of work, nonprofit industry, or community; the satisfaction of having done some good for the community; or the joy of sharing knowledge or experience.

Topics to cover in helping the client understand your capabilities include:

- *Describe your consulting experience and approach:* The client will be interested in seeing a résumé and a list of past clients or work experiences that prepare you to do the work. In addition, the client will want to talk about how you do the particular kind of work they want help with. What approaches do you tend to use? How have you approached this particular kind of project in the past?

- *Discuss values or conditions that guide your work:* Whether you work in a consulting group or solo, you may have a particular mission, specialty, or values that guide your work. Some consultants prefer working with antipoverty groups, or always address issues of pluralism, or prefer working with organizations who operate from an asset-building rather than problem-solving paradigm. You may prefer to work with organizations that operate with a shared power rather than a hierarchical decision-making model. Be clear about your preferences and values up front.

- *Describe what fee or value you want to receive in exchange for the work:* Tell the client what your fees are, and, if appropriate, the conditions under which they are negotiable. Find out what the client's budget is. Discuss alternative approaches to doing the work, and the possible cost of each approach. If you will be doing the work pro bono, clarify what you would like in place of a fee for doing the work, such as permission to use the client as a reference, time to sit in on board meetings to learn, or access to the organization's library.

The sample agenda for an initial client meeting (Figure 1 shown below) is a suggested outline for moving through Steps 1–3 in the contracting stage. It can be used either in a face-to-face meeting or as a guide for a telephone conversation.

The first three steps in the Contracting Stage lead up to a decision to proceed with either Step 4 (Develop a proposal or written agreement) or Step 5 (Decide whether to proceed with a consulting project).

Figure 1   **Agenda for an Initial Client Meeting**

---

1. Introductions

2. Clarify the client's concerns and goals
   - What does the client want help with?
   - What outcomes do they hope to accomplish?
   - What is their organization's mission and history?

3. Describe the consultant's background and experience
   - Past experience with similar organizations and type of work
   - Values and style preferences that might be relevant
   - Availability and rates, if appropriate

4. Determine whether there is mutual interest in further discussion

5. Explore specific aspects of the consulting project
   - Possible approach
   - Time frame
   - Division of labor between consultant and client
   - Cost

6. Define next steps
   - Is other information needed?
   - Do other people need to be part of the discussion?
   - Who will be making the decision, and by when?
   - What kind of proposal or documentation is needed?
   - When will the next discussion take place?

Step 3: Begin Developing the Consulting Relationship

There are two different and interrelated aspects to the consulting relationship: the formal or work relationship and the interpersonal relationship. The work relationship is normally outlined in the contract or agreement and describes the work to be done, who will do what, and how costs will be covered. As you work through the "formal" or work contract, you will also begin to develop a relationship with the client. The interpersonal relationship is more difficult to develop and define, and perhaps even more important than the formal agreement. It is most often understood and recognized in its absence—when you don't get along with someone, don't trust them, or sense guardedness or defensiveness. A productive consulting relationship requires openness and trust between the consultant and the client. It requires that both are able to question, challenge, and influence the other during the course of the work. Elements of the relationship that are important to clarify include what each of you wants from the other, how much humor and personal sharing is okay, and how formally you will address each other. This relationship is crucial to your ability to work in partnership with the client.

You will only start the relationship-building process in the first meetings with the client; your relationship will grow and become clearer as you proceed with the work. Issues to consider or discuss about the relationship during the contracting stage include:

- *Decide how information and feedback will be exchanged:* Suggest to the client that you discuss how you give each other feedback during the course of the consultation. You might ask: "How direct would you like me to be in sharing observations about the organization that may or may not be in the scope of work laid out in the consulting project?" "Are you interested in any observations I might have about you or your role in the organization?" You can also say, "I hope you will give feedback about my work and the impact of that work in the organization. Would you be willing to do that?" You might suggest setting a regular check-in time—a weekly meeting or phone call to see how things are going.

- *Clarify communication, reporting, and decision-making issues:* Who in the organization will be your contact person during the project? Will that person have the authority to make decisions that need to be made? If not, clarify how you will have access to the decision maker(s). If a group will be the decision maker, as is often the case with a community group or collaborative effort, will the client chair the meetings with you serving as a resource person, or does the client want you to run meetings to allow him or her to participate as a group member? Does the group function well in decision making?

Will decisions be made by consensus or vote? If the group functions well in decision making the project will take less time than if they often get bogged down in details or tangents. Who will you give reports to, and in what form would they like reports?

It's important to clarify who the client is, and get agreement about communications and reporting. I once had a client with whom I got in a fair amount of trouble. This organization has a high-powered corporate board and high-powered executive. I knew the board chair and executive fairly well. Although I saw them both regularly, I did most of my work with the executive. Once the president asked me about progress with the consulting project. I felt it was appropriate to brief him, at least generally, assuming that information was being shared between the two of them. After I briefed him, the president burst in upon the executive with information I had shared with him. He was very upset about the information. Unaware of all this when I next talked to the executive, I felt a little strain in her voice. I asked if there was anything else she would like to discuss. She told me what had occurred. I was totally amazed and felt terrible that I had caused the distress. I almost lost the client relationship. She said, "I know you know the president, but I am your client and I will be the one to share information with the board." I reassured her that in the future I would be careful to communicate only through the executive. The three of us clarified roles and communications, and it worked well after that. They have not engaged me again although both persons remain friends. They haven't indicated that this situation was the reason, but there is always a lingering question for me. Now, if there is any question about the lines of communication, I clarify this at the time of contracting. Many times I will have both the chair and executive in the contracting discussion. I also make sure they appoint a point person and get role definition clear.

— *Carol L. Barbeito, Ph.D., President*
Applied Research and Development
Institute International

- *Define the division of labor:* Who will do what during the consulting project? Will the client schedule meetings, send meeting notices, and write and distribute minutes or is this expected of the consultant? Who will arrange meeting rooms, do copying, and make arrangements with printers or other vendors? Who will write final reports or plans?

Step 4: Develop a Proposal or Written Agreement

Experienced consultants find that having a written agreement outlining the work to be done and agreements about steps, scheduling, products, fees, and billing is crucial to successful consulting work. This written agreement can take many forms, ranging from formal contracts, proposals, and letters of agreement to verbal agreements. A written agreement is always preferable to unwritten agreements for both the consultant and client. Sample proposals and letters of agreement are provided in Appendix B, Sample Consulting Proposals, on page 179.

Contracts can cover the entire scope of work to be done on a project, or can include only a first or second phase. Overall contracts are easier when a project is small or the consultant has a lot of experience in the kind of work to be done. With larger projects, or with inexperienced consultants who aren't sure what to expect after the second or third stage of the consulting process, it might be preferable to contract for the first two or three stages at the beginning, and then develop a second contract to cover the remaining work when the scope of work is clearer.

An important decision is whether you submit a proposal for an entire project, or for the first phase of a consulting project. I often submit proposals, an initial work plan, and cost estimates for the first phase, and wait until I know more to project the next phase. If I bid for a whole project I usually take a bath. It's important to build up trust and learn more about what is needed. Projects grow organically, and client needs change. What I want to do is help the client, whatever that might mean. So I end up revising the work plan several times, which helps the client respond to changing circumstances.

— *Diane Brown*
Non-Profit Assistance Group

Requests for proposal

Some organizations will issue a request for proposal (RFP) when they are seeking consulting assistance. The RFP will generally provide background information on the organization, the objectives to be met by the consultant, and details about methods, timing, and budget. With the RFP they invite proposals from several consultants.

Proposal content

Following is an outline of common sections of a consulting proposal or agreement.

- *Cover page* includes name of client; name of individual or organization preparing the proposal; and date submitted.

- *Background* includes events and circumstances leading to the development of the proposal; client's stated needs or concerns; and consultant's observations and understanding of the issues.

- *Project objectives* defines specific objectives to be achieved through the consulting effort.

- *Work plan* outlines the approach the consultant proposes to take; the steps involved and who is responsible for each; the time frame and target dates; and any follow-up steps.

- *Products* outlines deliverables, including instruments and reports (described in detail); meeting summaries and agendas; report production and distribution responsibilities; and statements of confidentiality and proprietary rights, if relevant.

- *Credentials* describes who is the lead consultant and other people who might work on the project; relevant experience and qualifications; and client references.

- *Budget* describes costs for completing the work using hourly, daily, or project basis; other direct costs that will be billed, such as printing, copying, or meeting space; and whether the costs listed are fixed, actual to a ceiling, or estimated.

- *Billing* describes when invoices will be sent (e.g., monthly, end of project); to whom bills will be sent; and who is responsible for payment, and to whom payments are made.

- *Signature page* includes space for authorized signatures by consultant(s) or organization submitting the proposal; client organization including board president and executive director; and organization responsible for payment if different from the client, and date.

Less formal than a proposal, a *letter of agreement* often outlines, at a minimum, the project objectives, work plan, products, budget, and billing portions of the above proposal outline. A letter of agreement is shown in Appendix B, Sample Consulting Proposals, on page 183.

Step 5: Decide Whether to Proceed with a Consulting Relationship

Both you and the client have a decision to make—whether to pursue working together. This decision can be reached quickly and simultaneously, or it can involve significant deliberation on one or both of your parts. Often the decision to proceed is made gradually. The client invites you to submit a proposal. You develop and submit the proposal. The client may be interviewing several consultants, or, you may need to go through a series of interviews. Or the client may need to get board or staff approval of their consultant selection.

On your side, you may need to consider how this project fits with your capabilities, availability, and goals. You may have to determine whether you can assemble needed resources—other consultants, research assistance, or support help.

At any time during Stage 1, you or the client might decide not to pursue a consulting relationship. They may decide to work with someone else, or you may decide that the work doesn't match your skills or availability. Keep in mind that the organization is still a prospective client, and that at some time in the future you might be able to work with them. This is an opportunity to provide a service to them such as referral to other possible consultants, a copy of an article that relates to their situation, or even a letter that thanks them for considering you for the work.

Or, you and the client mutually decide that there is a fit between their needs and your capabilities, and you reach agreement on all the details of the work that is to be done. You are both excited about proceeding. The only remaining tasks are to clarify what the next steps will be to begin the work and to communicate with anyone inside or outside the organization who might need to know that you will be engaged in this work with the organization.

Challenges in Stage 1

1. Deciding who the client is and whether you have the right client

Except in unusual circumstances, I contract with the board of a nonprofit or community organization. Even when the consulting work is at the staff or operational level in the organization, I will commonly ask for a meeting with the board chair and get the contract signed by both the executive director and board chair or president. Too many times I've contracted with the executive director as the client and found that the executive director was part of the dilemma that needed to be resolved. Without the board as the client, I have little leverage to influence the organization unless the executive director is open to feedback and change. Contracting at the staff level is appropriate when you are working within a large nonprofit or when the work you are doing is focused on a particular function, such as coordinating a special event or designing a new system.

The question of *who is the client?* becomes critical when you have to make strategic decisions in the consulting process. Some questions you will likely face include:

- Whom do I share diagnostic information with, and in what order?

- If I contract with a middle manager in a larger organization, and then find that some key positions, including the client's, could be eliminated, who is my client?

- What do I do if I find the organization is not performing at a level that produces a responsible swap of value between the public money invested and the results produced?

These dilemmas are discussed in more detail in later stages in this chapter.

I have learned through experience to contract with the highest possible level in the organization. I once contracted with the executive director of a small social service organization with a staff of ten. When I got into the project I realized I should've contracted with the board because at least part of the problem was the executive director. His performance was causing some serious problems in the organization. Because I had a contract with the director, I couldn't report to the board without his permission. I asked him if I could report my findings to the board. He said it was his job, and he didn't do it. I finally told him if he didn't talk to the board I had to stop working with him, that I couldn't meet my end of our contract relationship. The director at that point chose to terminate our consulting relationship. After this situation I almost always contract directly with the board, unless it is a large organization and the work is clearly at the operating level. But even then, I try to have a "client" one level up from the unit I'm working with.

— *Emil Angelica*
Amherst H. Wilder Foundation

I've learned how important it is to contract with a board and to involve the board in developing plans. I was a relatively inexperienced consultant when I was contacted by a young man who had started a small children's theater. He wanted to take the kids on tour and wanted advice on how to raise money to do that. I worked with the man and developed a plan that involved the active participation of the parents in raising the necessary funds. We held a meeting to present the plan to the parents. They were not particularly welcoming, and as I talked I noticed a growing stony silence in the room. I finished my presentation and asked for questions. As they began to talk, it dawned on me that I had made the mistake of not consulting them. Most human beings don't want to ask for money. If you are going to ask people to ask for money, or in fact do anything, you need to start meeting with them early on. These parents weren't sure they liked the director, the idea of their children touring, or me. It was a hostile group, and I ended up having to backpedal several blocks. This brought home for me the question of who I am working for. We are often contacted by a key staff person, but unless it is a real inside job, and there are few of those, a consultant needs to talk to the board immediately. That goes triple if volunteers will be asked to raise money.

— *Barbara Davis*
Independent Consultant

2. Entering a different culture

Every organization you enter has a unique culture—that is, its own history, norms, values, beliefs, and ways of operating. As a consultant your task is to learn about this culture and help the client find ways of doing things that will be congruent with, and effective within, their cultural framework. Many nonprofit organizations represent cultures that are entirely different from anything in your experience. These cultures may be based on economics, ethnicity, gender, values, or political, social, or geographic experience. Entry into these different cultures can be challenging.

During Stage 1 of the consulting process, you need to attend to three aspects of cross-cultural work:

A. Learn the history and cultural values of the group. Find out what's important in their culture—how decisions are made, how communications occur, how people deal with differences or conflict. Find out what their experience has been with consultants in the past and what you need to pay attention to so that you honor their cultural customs in the work you do.

B. Examine your own cultural background and beliefs and pay attention to assumptions you make or techniques you use that are based on your own cultural experiences or biases.

C. Decide what you need to learn or do to be effective, and ask for help with that learning as part of the consulting relationship.

In some cases, it may be important to the client to work with a consultant with the same cultural background; in other cases, the client might value a consultant from a different culture who can help them bridge cultures; or, cultural background may not be important. Raise the question early with the client. Bringing the topic into the open will serve you well in establishing a good working relationship throughout the project.

Sometimes we bridge cultures by paying attention to simple human needs. I was hired by a large corporation working on a venture to strengthen farming and food distribution systems and create jobs in the Arctic. My assignment was to increase cross-cultural understanding between the corporation and the people in the villages in the Arctic. On one trip in the Arctic I was sitting on the floor of a tent drinking coffee and talking with an Inuit woman when the Inuit farmers, who had been working outside, came in for dinner. Unknown to me, here was a sexual politics/cross-cultural trap and I was in trouble. My behavior meant one of two things to the Inuit Arctic farmers: either I was too dumb to know that a woman doesn't have anything important to say; or if I knew that, then I was intentionally slighting them as men by continuing to talk to her when I should have turned immediately to them. Consequently, as we all sat eating supper, they talked among themselves in their own language and ignored me. Later, the mosquitoes began to bite quite ferociously. I pulled mosquito repellent out of my work bag, put it on myself, and offered to pass it around the circle. They accepted it, put it on, and began to smile and engage me in English. I'm sure that until that moment they had no idea what they were going to do with a white, Lower-Forty-Eight consultant on an Arctic farm, who after all had already told them he didn't know how to fix the diesel tractor engine. However, once I popped out the mosquito repellent, I had something concrete to offer and we began the business of getting involved with each other.

— *Michael Groh*
Independent Consultant

I've learned that there are huge cultural differences in how people listen, learn, process information, and communicate. Face-to-face discussion is important when communicating across cultures; many people don't respond to letters and formalities. They want people to come to their house and meet with them there. I've been exploring Native American decision-making traditions and applying them to my work in the community. For example, a diverse group of people in our community has been meeting to probe problems that exist because of racial tensions and develop scenarios for creating a different community. We've created rules for dialogue, and use the Native American tradition of silence as part of the dialogue, giving people time to think for a couple of minutes before speaking.

— *Ruth Yellow Hawk*
Independent Consultant

When I was working in Borneo I lived in a building with three units. There was a family in one of the other units. When we met I told them that, since we are living so closely together, if there is any problem they should let me know. At one lunch break I had a splitting headache, and the neighbors brought music and speakers out on their porch and were playing it loudly. I asked them to turn it down a little in what I thought was a very polite way. They screamed, slammed the door, and wouldn't speak to me. After that, even people in the cafeteria wouldn't speak to me for a long time. I left for a while, and when I returned I brought back a gift for the child, and they invited me for a visit at the close of Ramadan (the fasting month). Suddenly, their coldness to me was over. What I learned was that I should've told someone else about my discomfort with their loud music. That person would have conveyed the message to the family, and we all would have saved face. I've learned that same lesson here working with executive directors of mutual assistance associations that serve Southeast Asian communities. That is how many people from Asian cultures handle conflict. They talk to someone else and never confront someone directly with a problem. In our culture we are direct and don't appreciate the subtleties and importance of indirect communication.

— *Pixie Martin*
Independent Consultant

3. Exploring possible hidden agendas

Consultants are often retained to help make hard decisions for the organization, such as how to cut expenses or reduce staffing levels, how to phase out a program, or whether to pursue a merger. At times key individuals in the organization can have expectations that aren't explicit, such as eliminating a weak performer, or getting the consultant to support a position that has already been decided by a subgroup in the organization. The more that some of these hidden agendas can be discussed at the beginning of the consulting project, the more effective the consulting project is likely to be.

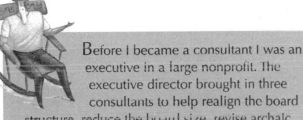

Before I became a consultant I was an executive in a large nonprofit. The executive director brought in three consultants to help realign the board structure, reduce the board size, revise archaic bylaws, and introduce technology. The organization had gone through rapid growth, the board and volunteers were out of touch with staff, and staff were out of sync with the volunteer leadership. The board/volunteer group habitually micromanaged and was resistant to change. Everything the executive director tried was blocked or rejected by the volunteers. Eventually the three consultants were fired by the executive director, under direction from the board. But a year of time and a lot of money was wasted on a consulting process that didn't go anywhere.

In reflecting on the situation, there were some dynamics operating that made it difficult for the consultants to be effective. Enormous hidden agendas weren't being talked about openly. The role of volunteers in the organization wasn't defined. The organization was spread out geographically, and communications were fragmented. And the board and volunteers had minimal involvement in the selection of, or contracting with, the consultants. The key steps that could've made a difference in this case would've been to engage the board and volunteer leadership in the change effort right at the beginning, and to make some of the hidden agendas explicit.

— *John B. McHugh*
McHugh Publishing and Consulting

4. Saying no

Many prospective consulting projects will come your way when you are experienced and have a track record. Some of these consulting projects will fit perfectly with your experience and skills, and you will readily accept the work. Other projects clearly don't fit with your strengths or availability, and you won't hesitate to decline them, often offering to assist the organization in finding another resource. A third category of prospective projects fits somewhere in between and can be trying to handle. You are attracted to the work for any number of reasons, including commitment to their mission, the benefits of affiliation with the organization, good money, or doing a favor for a friend. Yet you have a nagging feeling that you shouldn't take it on— maybe you're busy already, or you think the work has little hope of success, or it just doesn't feel right and you can't articulate what the issue is.

I've taken on many projects even when I knew, at some level, that I shouldn't be doing the work. In every case I ended up muddling or limping through the process, doing less than what I'm capable of. The client in those cases hasn't gotten the best I have to offer, and less than they deserve.

I've learned to listen to my heart and say no when I have doubts. Pay attention to the hesitation, the "yes, but . . ." when you consider accepting a consulting project. Unless you feel excited and confident about a new project, stop and assess what is going on with you. Turn down the project if things about it don't seem right.

A consultant needs to have clear criteria for the projects they take on and be willing to lose some projects. In one case, a previous client's board called us in to help with an executive search. We knew from our prior work with the organization that the former director left in part because of serious cash flow problems and the board's style. We knew that to work with this board, based on our ethical standards, we had to share our concerns with them. So we sat down with the board and said, "If we do an executive search, a good candidate will raise questions. We know about some of your past problems. We have to know how you will answer candidates' questions." So we posed all the hard questions about executive and governing roles, the financial condition of the organization, and the board's role in fund-raising. The board was frustrated with all our questions, but they talked about the actual situation of the organization, and accepted their share of responsibility for some of the past problems. They finally decided they didn't want to work with us, which was okay. If we hadn't been clear about what conditions were necessary in the organization and in our relationship with the client before we proceeded with developing a contract, we would've had a struggle throughout the project.

— *Larry Guillot, Executive Director*
Center for Management Assistance

Stage 1 Summary

In the contracting stage of the consulting process you have:

1. Learned about the organization and the work to be done
2. Helped the client understand your capabilities and goals as a consultant
3. Begun establishing a relationship with the prospective client
4. Developed a proposal or written agreement
5. Decided with the client whether to proceed with the consulting work, or terminated discussion about a consulting project

You are now poised to begin work with the organization. The foundation work you do in Stage 1 will to a large extent determine how successful you are throughout the rest of the consulting project. The written agreement you have developed is a road map for you and the organization or group as you proceed through the consulting project. And your ability to form a real partnership relationship with the client will determine how well you will be able to weather the challenges of the work ahead.

In the next section, Stage 2: Gathering and Analyzing Data, you will gather the information you need to assist the organization in bringing about desired changes.

STAGE 2: Gathering and Analyzing Data

The purpose of the second stage is to understand fully what the organization or group is hoping to accomplish and what will be needed for them to achieve their goals. Information is needed both by you, to understand the organization or group and their situation, and by the client, to help guide their decision making. In both cases, gathering and analyzing data is intended to move the client toward action that will address their challenges.

In the Contracting Stage, Step 1 suggested that you need to learn about the organization and the nature and scope of work to be done to decide whether to contract with the client, and to help you determine how to proceed with the work. The data collection you do in the first stage is preliminary—you learn just enough to make those decisions. In Stage 2: Gathering and Analyzing Data, you will do much more thorough data gathering and analysis to assist the client in forming and accomplishing goals.

In some cases data gathering will be brief—for example if the project is to facilitate a one-day board planning retreat or to design a promotional piece. In other projects the data collection may be more comprehensive, such as if you are asked to assist the organization with strategic planning or restructuring or to help them design a new program or technical process. The range of information needed will vary by the nature of the project.

Several methods of data collection are available to you, including records review, interviews, focus groups, surveys, and direct observation/experience. Each serves a different purpose and requires different skills. In this stage we will describe these methods of data collection and explore the advantages and disadvantages of each. Each of these data collection methods requires professional training. The purpose of providing an introduction to data collection is that it is necessary in most consulting work, and consultants need to know enough to advise clients to obtain resources to help with data collection that is beyond the consultant's level of training and experience.

Once you have collected needed information you will need to summarize it, analyze what implications it has for the project, and then share the information with the organization. Based on this information, decisions will then be made about how to proceed with the remainder of the project. This is also a good time to review your original contract agreement to make sure the anticipated project plan and budget are still appropriate.

Organizations often hire consultants to do data collection—it is time-consuming and requires specialized expertise often not available in the organization. Keep in mind, though, that this is your client's discovery process, not yours. And the act of obtaining and understanding new information is a powerful intervention that by itself can cause profound change in an organization or group. The steps that you move through in planning and executing the data collection, and the ways that you work in partnership with your client, will make a big difference in the choices the client makes later in their change effort.

Data collection can be a powerful intervention in conflict situations. I was asked to consult with a nonprofit professional training institute. They had a terrific conflict between the board and faculty about who ran the institute. It was very divisive. Our challenge was to find a way to get the groups talking together and get agreement on a new way of operating. We started by interviewing faculty, administrative staff, and board members to learn more about their concerns. But the key to finding common ground was in interviewing other similar institutes around the country and studying their bylaws. Everyone learned a lot, and we discovered several different governance models that could work. We started exploring some new ideas, such as having students and faculty serve on the board, and setting up a board affairs committee. Learning from other organizations and not trying to reinvent the wheel had great value for us. It gave everyone a common focus and reduced the tension and differences between the board and faculty.

— *William P. Hall*
Volunteer Consultant, Executive Service Corps of Chicago

A simple method of building the client's ownership of the information gathering process is to establish a task force or team from within the nonprofit or community group (or their constituents) to work with you in planning and implementing the data collection. This group will make key decisions during the process, work with you during the analysis, and be involved in the feedback process. You can also use members of the group or organization as interviewers or recorders in focus groups. As a general rule they should not interview or be in a focus group with people with whom they work or live—it will color their objectivity too much. Provide training and coaching to help them succeed.

Five steps will take you through Stage 2: Gathering and Analyzing Data. Each of these steps will be fully explored in the following section.

1. Decide what information is needed and how to get it

2. Communicate with various constituencies about the data collection

3. Gather needed information

4. Summarize and analyze information

5. Share information with the organization or group

Step 1: Decide What Information Is Needed and How to Get It

As mentioned earlier, the kind of information needed and the methods for collecting the information will vary widely from project to project. In some cases you may only have to meet with a couple of key people and review historical documents; in other situations you may have to organize massive studies of a community or an issue. In some cases the goal of your consulting project is to collect information and not work further with the client in using the information for their planning or decision making. In those situations, your consulting project will end after Stage 2. In either case the general steps are the same:

- **Determine information needed by you and the client to achieve their goals**

  The kind of information needed will vary by the nature and scope of the project you are working on. If you are working on management issues within an organization you may need to collect information about past management practices, future organizational plans, or current staff attitudes and perceptions about the organization. If you are assisting an organization with planning for the future you will need to consider a broader range of information including the organization's history, services, and performance, current capabilities and vulnerabilities, trends and opportunities in their line of work, the outcomes they hope to produce through their programs and services, and attitudes and opinions from their various constituencies. If you are working with a neighborhood organization or a community collaborative you may need to collect even broader information about the community and the various organizations or constituencies addressed by the group. Figure 2 on page 40 illustrates a range of possible kinds of information that may be needed.

Figure 2	Kinds of Information That May Be Needed
Information about the organization or group	• Mission • History • Audience served • Programs and services • Board: membership/representation, structure, role, relationship with executive, advisory board • Results or performance • Future goals and objectives • Intended service outcomes • Staff structure and leadership • Management practices and systems • Finances: financial performance, challenges, systems, operating budget, revenue sources, funding patterns • Legal structure • Key challenges and opportunities
Information about the industry or group	• National or local trends • Relevant public policies • Best-practice models • Expert or opinion leader input • Competitor and ally information
Information about the people— in the organization or community	• Needs of board, staff, volunteers • Culture—values and beliefs • Expectations and preferences • Assets and talents • Demographic profile • Opinions about issues
Information about the neighborhood, community, or broader society	• Social conditions or trends • Economic conditions or trends • Demographic characteristics • Political concerns or trends • Technological trends • Funding resources or patterns

Framing your inquiry right will have a great deal to do with the overall success of your project. This is especially important if your consulting expertise is in one of the many technical areas such as marketing, personnel, or housing production. The presenting problem—how to improve outreach to people of color in the neighborhood or how to have more impact with a housing rehab program—may seem clear. But often contributing factors in the organization and its management practices affect the organization's performance in the technical area. For example:

> *Southside Development Partnership was trying to have more impact in housing rehab. The assumption was that they didn't have the right program design. The consultant researched the organization's current housing programs, community needs, and other program models that might work. But the critical factor turned out to be that the organization's board was composed of business owners who had a strong value for business development and placed little emphasis on housing programs. Because of this they historically passed up opportunities for partnership with other housing resources and repeatedly vetoed ideas for enhancing or expanding their housing rehab efforts. The consultant and staff gathered useful information on best practices, created an artfully designed housing rehab program, and obtained board approval for it, but it was never implemented because the board never supported start-up of the program. The consultant had never talked to the board about their interest in, and commitment to, housing, or questioned whether they viewed housing as a central focus of their mission.*

In this situation, the consultant and staff hadn't framed their data collection as comprehensively as they should have. They missed asking the board what was behind their past vetoes of housing development efforts.

- **Determine who has the information that you need**

  Often an organization or group will already have much of the information you need. Or the information may exist elsewhere in the community or another organization, such as with school districts, city planning departments, or research organizations. However, in many cases information about people's hopes, visions for the future, or opinions about an issue are needed. For each kind of information you have to determine who has the information and how many people or sources you need to ensure reliability of the data. For example, in a consulting project with a neighborhood collaborative working on economic development, the information and source list looked like this:

Kind of information	Sources
Historical information, current membership, structure, budget, projects, and plans	• *Existing records*
Information about other related public and private efforts	• *Ten collaborative members* • *Six other community and government leaders*
Information about community needs and ideas about future direction	• *Sixty collaborative members* • *Fifty citizens* • *Twenty-five community leaders* • *Twenty-five business representatives* • *Twenty-five organizational / institutional leaders*
Future funder interests	• *Eight local foundations and corporations*

• **Decide how you will gather the needed information**

Methods of data collection will vary depending on what information is needed, the number and accessibility of sources of information, the time and money available to collect the information, your skill and experience with different forms of data collection, and the prevailing norms and political considerations in the community or organization. Your choice of data collection methods may also be influenced by historical, cultural, or political factors such as whether a large community survey was recently conducted, in which case doing another one might be confusing or irritating to the community. Or, with hot issues simmering in the organization, interviews would be more effective than a survey to understand the depth of concerns. Or, with a large number of Southeast Asian residents in the neighborhood, interviews by a Southeast Asian would have the best chance to get a good response.

Numerous books have been written on data collection methods, and many research professionals are available to work with nonprofit organizations. This section is intended to be only a brief overview of the choices that a consultant has. Further resources can be found in Appendix A, Resources, on page 163.

The choice of data collection methods needs to be decided jointly by you and the client; approval of the data collection design belongs to your client, but unless they have some expertise in research, they will rely heavily on your recommendations. Your job as a consultant is to educate the client about the different data collection methods and their pros and cons, connect the client with additional resources if that is needed, and prepare the data collection design and materials for final approval by the client.

Five methods of data collection are most commonly used: records review, interviews, surveys, focus groups, and direct observation or experience. These methods can be used alone but work best in combination; for example, you could conduct a survey in a telephone interview, or survey one group and conduct interviews with another group. Following is an introduction to each of the methods. Figure 3 on page 49 summarizes the advantages and disadvantages of three of the methods.

Records review

Records review involves studying current or historical information that exists in written form. In working with an organization it might involve studying their performance or production over time to determine patterns or trends. In working with a community group it might involve studying census tract data to derive key population, employment, housing, or mobility information to be used in planning. Records review can also involve review of literature to understand the industry context or trends. Records review can be done by the consultant or by a member of the group or organization.

Interviews

Interviews are useful for obtaining individual opinions or perceptions about an issue and for gathering information from sources located at a distance. They allow the consultant to explore topics in depth and probe for more information on critical issues. There are several design issues to consider in using interviews for data collection:

- Interviews can be conducted face-to-face or via telephone; they can be with an individual or a small group. Although face-to-face interviews will give you more information and allow you to use visual aids, they can be time-consuming for you and the interviewee. Telephone interviews, especially when the interviewee has a copy of the questions ahead of time, allow you to reach more people in less time.

- Interviews can be conducted by the consultant or by a member of the group or organization. A consultant or person outside the organization or group will be more objective in hearing and reporting interview information. However, in some circumstances, an interview conducted by a member of the client system can serve to build a relationship with a key constituent such as a funder or potential partner.

- Interviews require careful preparation and design to be effective. Interview questions should be thought through carefully, both for wording and sequencing. Interviewees need to know why they are being interviewed and what questions will be asked. They also need to know how the information will be used—whether their responses will be attributed to them or reported anonymously in summary form with other responses. Interviewees also need to know if they will see summary information from the interviews, or a report on how the group or organization has used the information collected.

- Interview guides are useful to ensure consistency, especially if more than one person will be conducting interviews. Interview guides often contain a script that describes how you will introduce the purpose of the interview, specific questions to be asked, probing questions to gain more information, and closing comments.

Surveys

Surveys are useful for obtaining information from a large number of people fairly efficiently. They can be used to get input on a wide range of topics, from individual or family characteristics to perceptions of community need to feedback on services received. A well-designed and administered survey can provide valuable information that is credible to many audiences. A poorly designed and administered survey can result in useless information, little information, information suspect because of unclear wording of questions, and a waste of money. In other words, use caution in your use of surveys. Whenever possible rely on advice from someone trained in their design and use. But don't avoid the use of surveys—they can be invaluable tools in data collection. Key factors to keep in mind include:

- Be very clear about what you want to learn through the survey, and word your questions carefully. A survey is only as good as the questions, and the same question can be worded in many ways. Be sure you ask for exactly what you need to know. Test your questions on several people to find out how they answer them and whether you are getting the kind of responses you intended.

- Consider carefully whether to ask open-ended, multiple-choice, or scaled-response questions. Open-ended questions will provide more detailed information but will be harder and more time consuming to tabulate and summarize and are a disincentive to many respondents. Multiple-choice questions are easier to tabulate but may limit the range of possible responses too much. Scaled response questions such as those using a scale of 1 to 5 will give information about relative opinion or experience. A mixture of question types is usually effective and necessary. Mailed surveys should avoid the use of multiple open-ended questions. They tend to depress the response rate.

- Consider the format and length of a survey that might appeal to your audience. Some people will toss a survey aside if it is too long, often over one page. The layout should be welcoming, with clear instructions for completing and returning the survey. Cash or gift incentives can increase the response rate by as much as 20 percent.

Focus Groups

Focus groups are highly structured group meetings that obtain feedback or solicit ideas on a specific topic or concept. Most focus groups involve a small number of participants, usually six to twelve, and explore a limited number of questions during a one- to two-hour session. Focus groups require a skilled facilitator who can keep the discussion lively and on topic, and a human or mechanical recorder. Focus groups are normally led by someone outside the organization or group. In some cases, when it is unlikely to inhibit the discussion, one or two members of the organization or group are allowed to observe to get the flavor of the discussion. Design issues to consider in using focus groups include:

- Select a small number of people to participate who have some characteristics in common; for example, all have benefited from the work of the group, or all of them are professionals in a similar line of work, or none of them knows anything about the work of the group. Mixing audience characteristics makes facilitation more difficult and the data more confusing to analyze but is sometimes done intentionally to get a range of opinions.

- Give the participants background information in advance of the session so they are clear about the purpose and know what to expect when they arrive.

- Just as with interviews or surveys, plan carefully what questions you will ask.

Facilitation Hints When Leading Focus Groups

1. Use standard tools for running effective meetings. Start with an agenda with times allotted for various activities. Adhere to the agenda, summarizing each item as you complete it to check for understanding.

2. Focus on three to four key questions to get in-depth responses. Group discussion takes more time than we usually anticipate. Be prepared to probe for underlying ideas.

3. Vary the method of asking questions and the response method to relieve boredom and accommodate different styles among participants. Ask some open-ended questions for group discussion; ask some forced-choice or multiple-choice questions and allow people to write their answers on a 3" x 5" card and turn them in anonymously; ask for demographic information in writing to avoid embarrassing participants.

4. Use a flip chart to record participant comments so people can see that you understood them. When recording comments, use participants' words exactly, or ask permission to rephrase their com-ments. Periodically check to make sure you are hearing correctly what they are saying. You may also want to tape the conversation to make sure you hear everything. If you do this, get a signed release giving you permission to tape.

5. Keep the discussion on track and on time for each question you are asking. Be prepared to interrupt long-winded people (diplomatically) or to mediate if a difference of opinion arises that distracts the group.

6. Ensure that all participants have an opportunity to contribute their thoughts. If some people dominate and others are quiet in open discussion, suggest moving around the table for everyone to contribute one idea at a time.

7. Summarize follow-up steps at the end. Clarify if you will be sending participants a summary of information or a report on how the information was used.

8. Always send thank-you letters to focus group participants.

Direct observation or experience

Direct observation and consultant experience is often overlooked or minimized as a data collection method. Certainly it doesn't have the face validity that other methods do. But it is a way of providing the consultant with valuable information. Things that can be observed include group process in a staff, board, or community meeting; the environment within an office or neighborhood; relationships between people; or the subjective impact of an exhibit or production, promotional material, or planning documents produced by a group.

Consultant experience might include such things as how the group or organization treats you, how they manage your contract, how honest or open they are in exploring issues, or how they respond to your feedback. Some of the most effective interventions I've made have been based on my own feelings about a situation that I've shared with a client. Telling a client that you are uncomfortable with the unexpressed conflict in a meeting, or that you were angry when they canceled two meetings in a row with you and wasted your time, can be powerful.

Direct observation and consultant experience are the most subjective form of data collection but also can be the most potent. Whether we are aware of it, we begin forming judgments about the group or organization from the first moment we talk on the phone or meet the client. Becoming conscious of our observations and using them as data rather than reacting to them personally is a valuable skill.

Earlier we looked at a community economic development collaborative that needed several kinds of information from multiple sources. Using that same example, the chart below shows what data collection methods were selected to gather the needed information.

Kind of information	Sources	Methods
Historical information, current membership, structure, budget, projects, and plans	• Existing records	• Records review
Information about other related public and private efforts	• Ten collaborative members • Six other community and government leaders	• Individual interviews conducted by members of the collaborative
Information about community needs and ideas about future direction	• Sixty collaborative members • Fifty citizens • Twenty-five community leaders • Twenty-five business representatives • Twenty-five organizational/institutional leaders	• Written survey sent to collaborative members and citizens • Six focus groups, two each for community leaders, business representatives, and organizational leaders, conducted by a consultant
Future funder interests	• Eight local foundations and corporations	• Individual interviews conducted by members of the collaborative

Notice that this group used multiple data gathering methods to get information. Using more than one method is useful to verify patterns and trends in responses and to make up for some of the deficiencies inherent in any one method.

- **Design your data collection tools and administrative procedures.**

  You have some homework now before beginning the actual data collection. Two tasks are key to success: crafting the right questions and instruments to get the information you want, and setting up the logistics to administer the data collection process.

  The kind of questions you ask and how you ask them will vary depending on the data collection method you are using. In general, ask questions in the simplest possible language; ask only what you need to know and tell people how you want them to respond. If you want a yes or no answer, give them only those options. If you want a lengthy brainstormed list, tell them that. If you want their two best ideas, give them space or time for only two responses. Test your questions before administering them. (After I've formatted my questions I often test them on several people to see if they respond in the way I want them to.)

  Decide how you will administer the data collection. The key here is to organize, organize, organize! Establish a timeline and responsibilities for every step in the process and make sure people stick to them. Decide what letters need to be sent to participants, then draft and edit them carefully. Decide who will do mailings, who will schedule meetings, who needs to be at every meeting, who will receive information and in what format, and who will tabulate information and in what format. Make sure that everyone involved in the data collection process is on board with this plan.

In Step 1 you decided what information is needed and how to get it. You are now ready to invite people to participate in the data collection process.

Step 2: Communicate with Various Constituencies about the Data Collection

Once you have decided what data collection methods to use and have designed the appropriate instruments, interviews, or focus groups, you need to communicate with the people you will be asking to contribute information. This communication, the invitation to participate and assist the organization or group, can be done by phone with a small group, or by letter. In all cases the invitation should be made by a representative of the organization, not by the consultant. Following are some steps to remember as you invite people to contribute information.

- **Explain why information is being collected and by whom**

  Tell people why you are gathering information and what you are hoping to achieve. If people will participate in only a portion of the data collection, let them know that other data collection efforts are going on

---

Advantages and Disadvantages of Data Collection Methods   Figure 3

Interviews

Advantages

- high response rate
- more personal approach/builds trust
- can get more in-depth information
- easier to understand than written responses
- can uncover hidden agendas
- advantage of seeing nonverbal cues (if in person) or verbal cues (if on phone)

Disadvantages

- time-consuming and costly
- difficult to standardize responses
- lacks anonymity
- risk of interviewer bias
- requires ability to take notes fast or tape and transcribe
- can get off track
- people may not be completely honest
- not good for some cultures

Mailed Surveys

Advantages

- can gather a lot of data
- can get input from broad audience
- can be less expensive than time-based method
- can get norm-based information
- anonymous
- easy to compile responses

Disadvantages

- risk of low response rate
- risk of getting response from verbal minority
- requires time and expert skill to prepare and tabulate survey
- information may not be clear, relevant, honest
- one-way communication
- no way to follow-up, probe
- 6-8 week turnaround time
- not good for some cultures

Focus Groups

Advantages

- quick results
- has face validity
- able to probe, get in-depth information
- variable sample size
- can key off group dynamics
- advantage of seeing body language

Disadvantages

- requires trained facilitator
- less control due to group dynamics
- people hard to assemble and schedule
- limited number of questions can be asked
- no anonymity
- complex data—hard to analyze
- potential for "group think" may corrupt results
- requires ability to take notes fast or tape and transcribe
- not good for some cultures

---

to supplement the part they will be participating in. Tell them that as a result of the data collection, you hope to have a better understanding of the neighborhood council's work, or a plan for the future.

- **Tell people that their participation is important**

  For most people, the chance to have their concerns heard and influence the future direction of the community or organization is enough. Others may be extremely busy or feel that their opinions are not important. Some may need to hear that every resident in the neighborhood is important to planning for the future. These people will need some encouragement or incentive. Some community groups have found that serving food or providing child care, transportation, or interpreters at a community meeting draws more people. Others have tried with success offering incentives or premiums such as a raffle, a copy of a book, subscription to a newsletter, or a potted herb for their garden.

- **Tell people what will be discussed**

  If people are being invited to participate in interviews or focus groups, you will want to tell them, at least generally, what the purpose of the session is.

- **Alert people if advance preparation is needed**

  Provide participants with background reading if it is important that they know something ahead of time, for example, if you want their reaction to a document or specific product. Also let them know whether you want them to prepare answers ahead of time or respond spontaneously.

- **Explain how the information will be used**

  One of the most commonly asked questions by survey respondents is whether their responses will be attributed to them or reported anonymously in summary form with other responses. This decision should be made ahead of time by the client, communicated to respondents, and honored at all steps in the data collection and reporting process. See Figure 4, Reporting Information, for definitions of commonly used information disclosure options.

- **Discuss when and how people need to respond**

  Tell people what the timeline is and how they need to respond. If you need to receive a survey by a particular day, tell them they need to postmark it by a certain day or fax it by a particular time. If at all possible offer them optional ways of responding.

- **State whether people will see a summary of the information or get feedback on how the information has been used by the organization or group**

  Let participants know whether they will see the results of the effort, and if so, when and how. Most people will be more inclined to participate if they will see a copy of the final report. The incentive for them is to see how their perceptions or opinions compare with those of other people.

You have carefully planned your data collection process and communicated with everyone who will participate. You are now ready to begin collecting information.

Reporting Information   Figure 4

There are three ways you can handle information you gather: keep it **confidential,** relay the information **anonymously,** or **attribute** it to its source. Following is a discussion of each approach.

Confidentiality—a commitment not to communicate information that you hear. People may ask you if they can tell you something "off the record." Making a commitment to confidentiality may make it possible to hear information you wouldn't otherwise hear. However, some information must be shared, such as evidence of improper actions, since it can create liability for your client. Try to avoid making a commitment to confidentiality when collecting data for an organization.

Anonymity—a commitment not to reveal in any way the source of a particular item of information. This means that you will report the information that you hear but will change language so the use of certain words or incidents can't be ascribed to a particular person or group, or that you will present information so that individual opinions are generalized or summarized with other opinions to avoid revealing the source. Participants in data collection are often given a commitment of anonymity. This should be decided with your client at the beginning of data collection.

Attribution—identifying information as coming from particular individuals or groups, often reported as direct quotes. Always obtain permission to attribute a comment publicly to someone, or let people know in advance that their comments may be quoted. Some consultants use a release form when gathering information from individuals.

Step 3: Gather Needed Information

In this step you implement the data collection plans you carefully laid out in Steps 1 and 2. By the end of Step 3 you will probably have a mountain of information that you will need to summarize and analyze. Following are some challenges to keep in mind during this information gathering step.

- **Focus on information relevant to your purpose**

  As you are gathering information it is important to keep in mind what your consulting project will accomplish and what information you need to accomplish that goal. Keep that focus as you collect information. You will get a lot of information, some of which is relevant to your purpose and some of which is not. At times you will also get information that is surprising or unexpected, some of which might be relevant and some not. Look for the kernels of wisdom, the key issues that will help the client make progress.

- **Collect enough information to ensure credibility**

  Two focus groups involving twenty-five people will not likely produce information considered representative of a neighborhood with a diverse population of twelve thousand. A survey involving five hundred people may have more credibility. If sample size is an issue in data collection you may want to consult a professional researcher for guidance.

- **Use experienced resources to assist you if you are trying a data collection method for the first time**

  Effective data collection requires artful design and execution. If you have limited experience in a method that the organization wants, consider seeking assistance from someone with more experience.

- **Conduct the data collection in a way that models norms and behaviors desired in the future by the organization or group**

  The act of collecting data is itself a powerful intervention in the life of an organization, neighborhood, or community group. Through it hopes are created, expectations are changed, new behaviors are experienced, and commitments for the future are made. Every element in the design and execution of data collection will send a message to participants about the client's values and beliefs. If a neighborhood group doesn't survey diverse representatives in the neighborhood, their implied message is that they don't value diversity. If feedback about one unit in an organization is shown to other departments before the original unit gets to see it, they feel disrespected and devalued. Make sure the data collection and feedback process is inclusive, open, and respectful of all people.

Once you have finished collecting information you move to the next step, which is to summarize and analyze the information.

Step 4: Summarize and Analyze Information

Now that you have collected information you have the task of transforming the raw data into useful information that will guide the group to effective action. This can be done by the client alone, the consultant alone, or the client and consultant together. Usually the consultant has a lead role in analyzing information, but the client needs to be involved enough so that they "own" the information.

Three tasks are involved in this process, including summarizing raw data, analyzing the data, and preparing a summary report.

- **Summarize raw data**

   Your summary of data may be as simple as a listing of what you heard, grouped in categories so that it is easily read and digested by your client; or it may be a complex summary of information heard from different constituencies, or from groups with different characteristics. Have your client decide the desired format for the information before you begin summarizing the information. Some want the original documents (flip chart sheets and returned surveys, for example); some want a rewritten list of verbatim comments from original documents; and some want only to see a summary of raw data. If you have agreed to keep the identity of respondents confidential, do not provide information to the client that would allow them to identify a particular respondent. Try to present information in readable language and formats that will focus attention on a few key points. A list of twenty-seven issues is overwhelming; grouping those into five themes will make them easier to digest and work with for the client. If you are providing a statistical analysis, a table or chart is sometimes easier to read than narrative.

- **Analyze data to determine meaning or implications for client**

   Analyzing data involves figuring out what it means, what is important, and why it is important. Normally this is done based on a predefined format or theoretical framework, often stated as part of your contract with the client. Examples of data analysis formats include:

   - Description of strengths, weaknesses, and opportunities for improvement or change

   - Breakdowns of descriptive information according to relevant demographic characteristics (such as differences between men and women)

   - Findings (raw data summarized) and implications

   - Comparison of the data with a theoretical model for how people, groups, organizations, neighborhoods, or systems function (for example, you might describe how the data fits with a model describing the stages of organizational evolution)

   - Diagnostic analysis of why conditions reported in the data might exist

   - Analysis to determine occurrence of factors with statistical significance

Data analysis will look different for different types of consulting projects. For example:

Type of data collected	Analytic framework used
Community opinion about neighborhood strengths, problems, and future needs	Frequency of each idea. Ideas expressed most often are considered most descriptive of community opinion.
Staff attitudes about pay, benefits, and working environment	Frequency of opinions expressed. May also be compared to national norms if information is available.
Survey of national teenage pregnancy prevention programs to determine best-practice models	Comparison of different program components and outcomes.
Staff opinion and historical information regarding organizational performance	Organizational systems model applied to key issues raised.

- **Prepare summary report**

    If your data collection process was "quick and dirty" (for example, you called five board members prior to planning a board retreat), you are unlikely to prepare a formal report summarizing what you heard from them, or your report may be a one-page list of the ideas expressed. However, for consulting projects with more involved data collection, you may need to prepare a more formal summary report.

    If the amount of detail and the format for your summary report is negotiated with the client *before* you write it, you will save significant time and energy. You may need to prepare more than one form of your report for different audiences, with more or less detail. Data collection reports typically have some or all of the following sections:

    - *Executive summary:* A very brief summary of the major sections in the report, usually on one to two pages. An executive summary is intended to be a quick summary of key issues as either an introduction to the detailed report or for those who won't read the full report.

    - *Table of contents:* Important if the document is long or has many sections.

- *Background:* Description of what led up to the study and what the organization hopes to accomplish. This section may also note who conducted the data collection.

- *Methodology:* Description of data collection timeline and process, methods used, and number participating or return rate.

- *Findings:* Summary of what was learned in the data collection. The body of the report usually contains a summarized version; detail is usually put in the appendix.

- *Conclusions or implications:* What the data mean. Summary of issues or opportunities that the group or organization might address.

- *Appendices:* Detailed information or analysis from your data collection. May include one or more of the following: verbatim survey or focus group responses; statistical comparison between different groups; list of people who contributed opinions; names of members of task force who orchestrated the data collection.

When you have completed your analysis and written a summary report you are ready to move on to Step 5: Share Information with the Organization or Group.

Step 5: Share Information with the Organization or Group

Confronting new information about a group or organization is much the same as looking in a mirror. We get new information, and our view of reality is challenged, whether we like the reflection or not. Feeding information back to a group requires careful planning and artful execution to make it a learning, growthful experience.

Plan the feedback process carefully. Decisions about what to present, how to present it, who should be involved, and how to help the group move from understanding the information to making decisions about their future are all important in this step. Following are some considerations when planning and executing a data feedback process.

- **Decide how to follow-up with those who contributed information**

   Encourage your client to consider sending those people from whom you collected information either an executive summary of the information collected or a copy of the full report if sharing the information doesn't violate a commitment to confidentiality.

- **Decide how to present information to the client system**

  If you are sharing information with multiple individuals or groups, decide what information you will share with each, and the sequence of the presentations. If data contains sensitive material, I will usually share it with the board and executive director before sharing it with staff. It is ideal to provide staff with the same full report as the board, but at times because of confidential personnel information or other data that may have legal implications for the organization, it is wise to abbreviate the staff report or omit some information entirely.

  If you have involved people in the neighborhood or organization in the data collection, use them to help present information. Or, if you have presented information to the board and executive director, try to involve them in presenting the information to staff. Remember that it is their data, and the more they talk about it the more they will understand and use it.

- **Prepare materials and visual aids**

  Use visuals, pictures, and conceptual models to illustrate your analysis, as well as words and written reports. One or two pictures or images will stay with a group longer, and help a group come to agreement faster, than the best written report. Supplementing written material with images and visuals will also allow you to tap into a variety of learning styles in the group.

- **Decide whether to send information to participants before the meeting**

  If the report is lengthy with complex information you may want to send it ahead if there is a likelihood that people will read it. However, if the report contains sensitive information, you may want people to hear it explained fully before they see it in written form.

- **Plan the feedback meeting**

  Feedback meetings are crucial in building the capacity of the group or organization to absorb and utilize the new information and understandings from the information gathered, and then to move to an action mode. Chances are you have lived with the information for some time. For members of the organization or group, much of the information will be new. Be careful not to move them too quickly into thinking about future action or decisions. Allow them time to absorb the information, massage it, and add to it.

It is critical to get clear about reporting and communications expectations at the beginning of a project. In one situation, after gathering and analyzing loads of data, an inexperienced consultant prepared a feedback report and mailed a copy to the executive director and the board president, confident that the facts would be seen as learning opportunities. Imagine his dismay upon receiving a phone call from the executive director. "How dare you send a copy to my board president and promote board meddling in day-to-day issues? And how dare you send a copy of the report in general mail? This stuff is confidential! My staff opened it and the report dropped out, in plain sight of all the staff. I demand an immediate meeting to go over factual errors in this report and to have you apologize to my board president and key staff for misrepresenting the issues." At first glance, the consultant wanted to write off this client's sensitivity as part of the organizational growth issues being addressed. But the consultant finally concluded that internal management portions of the report should have been reported to the executive director only; and a separate version of the report dealing with policy issues should have been prepared for the board. The consultant did not need to change the substance of the report, but rather, renegotiate the amount of detail which needed to be provided to the various constituents.

— *Karen Simmons*
Director, LaSalle University Nonprofit
Center and President, Nonprofit
Management Association

In planning the feedback meeting you will likely encounter a "make it quick and clear" mentality from the client. Boards typically want to spend thirty to sixty minutes at most at a board meeting hearing a presentation. That may be appropriate if the presentation is for information only and is not relevant to the board's level of decision making. However, if the information has to do with the board's functioning or future direction of the organization, both clearly within the board's role, more time is needed.

Depending on the scope and complexity of data and the importance of it to the organization's future, a feedback meeting, or a succession of meetings, will need two to eight hours, including identifying and prioritizing key issues to be addressed. Figure 5 on page 58 shows a sample feedback meeting agenda. Some general hints about feedback meetings include:

- Consider having someone from the group or organization who has been involved in the data collection do the reporting. You may have to coach them on how to present the information.

- Understand your audience, their style, and their special needs such as language or sign interpreters or time constraints because of other commitments.

- Don't give people a report and then expect them to pay attention to your page-by-page presentation. If you want their attention on a presentation, withhold the written report until you are finished.

- Allow enough time for the group to digest data, discuss implications, and work through any feelings generated by the information.

- Provide more time for discussion than for presentation. Discussion needs to include three components—questions about and clarification of the data, discussion of what the data means and how people will react to it, and discussion of what the data's implications are for the group or organization in the future.

- If at all possible try to engage your client in prioritizing issues raised in the data. This involvement will greatly increase their understanding of the data and their commitment to moving to action.

- If you are providing recommendations, put them on a separate piece of paper that you give the client only *after* the client has discussed their ideas about what to do. At that point you can use them to see if there are any gaps in the issues identified by the client.

Figure 5   **Typical Agenda for a Feedback Meeting**

---

1. Introductions

2. Review project history and outcomes
   - What prompted the data collection
   - Desired outcomes or results

3. Describe the scope and methodology of the data collection
   - Data collection methods and timetable
   - Sources of data, including response rates
   - Feedback process: who has heard and will hear information

4. Describe findings and conclusions
   - Clarify information as needed

5. Discussion (in small groups if more than ten to fifteen people are present)
   - Does the data and analysis make sense? What is most useful? What is most surprising?
   - What are the three to five most critical issues we need to address?
   - What are the implications for future plans?

6. Decide on the most important critical issues to address
   (If Step 5 was done in small groups, have the groups report and then identify common themes in their reports.)
   - Summarize and prioritize key issues that need to be addressed
   - Identify implications for the future

7. Define next steps
   - Decide whether the information reported is public or is to be kept confidential
   - Clarify follow-up communications with other groups or people regarding information (especially those in the organization who missed the meeting)
   - Decide next steps and timetable in planning process

Challenges in Stage 2

1. Collecting data with different cultural groups

With some cultures surveys work well; in others you will need a face-to-face interview to get information. Some cultural groups will only feel comfortable talking in a group setting where there is safety in numbers. You may be working with a group where English is not spoken as a native language; in this case you will need to bring in a facilitator or interpreter who speaks the native language. In some cultures, women will not speak unless their supervisor or husband is present; in others women will speak only if a woman is present.

Countless books and articles are available describing culture-specific characteristics of various cultural groups. This is useful background information to have, but often it contains generalizations about complex cultural groupings. These generalizations may or may not be appropriate with your client group. In addition, factors other than ethnicity are important in data collection such as age, gender, economics, or religion. The point is that you will need to work in partnership with your client to select the best way to collect information. If at all possible, find a way for someone from the organization or group to work with and guide you on data collection and possibly help collect the information.

Consulting with Asian organizations is very different than with mainstream organizations. Face-to-face relationships are important, and the formal support of the executive is necessary. With several clients I've struggled to get staff to work with me and give me information. I've discovered that I have to get the executive to approve the project formally and then meet together with me and staff to let staff know it is okay to talk to me. Then I have to spend time talking with staff about things that are familiar to them, and give them examples of what we will be talking about. Only then do they become comfortable enough to talk. In the Asian culture, you can't just call someone on the phone or send a letter and expect a response unless you have a prior relationship with them or are a funder.

You have to meet with them face-to-face to explain why it is important that you work together. When they know you really care, they will trust you. If an organization asks for my help and I don't have the skills or time, I can't say no or give them the name of another consultant. I'm obligated to set up a meeting with the client and a different consultant; then they will work with the other consultant. Most consultants have to plan extra time when they consult with Asian organizations. There is little separation between business life and social life. The client will invite you to social events, and you have to participate. If you do, they will trust you more and tell you more.

— *Somly Sitthisay*
Amherst H. Wilder Foundation

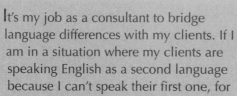

It's my job as a consultant to bridge language differences with my clients. If I am in a situation where my clients are speaking English as a second language because I can't speak their first one, for example, Hmong or Inupiat, I need to remind myself to slow down and simplify as much as possible. I try to "hear" the next sentence in my mind, mentally editing it ahead of time for jargon or words that will be tricky for them to process. I can't speak English in a manner that assumes that my clients think in English as easily as I do. In my work in Quebec with the French Canadians, most of the meetings are bilingual. Sometimes they are in French, sometimes in English. When in English, I slow down particularly for those who do not speak English as their mother tongue. When they speak French, I try to sit next to an English-speaking person who will whisper short translations in my ear when he thinks I need them. The group will summarize in English whatever they think I need to know. If they don't think I need a running translation of what's going on in French they don't tell me. This is fine. One of the skills I've learned is how to watch body language and facial expressions, and feel vibes. I like to encourage a client to discuss as much as possible in their own first language, and have it be my challenge to figure out how to help them.

— *Michael Groh*
Independent Consultant

This is an example of the importance of careful design and planning when working with people in different cultures. Several years ago we were hired to assess the effectiveness of services provided to people with AIDS. Our information sources were predominately low income with widely ranging ethnicity, gender, and ages. They were people at risk, intravenous drug users, sex trade workers—people who were hard to contact and nervous about sharing information. We had a dozen different demographic subgroups to reach such as homeless gay men, female prostitutes, and African American female drug users. Our challenge was to design a data collection process that would effectively recruit people and make them comfortable sharing information. We designed a two-pronged approach. First, we hired "community research advocates" who were either members of a specific targeted community or worked for an organization serving those communities to recruit people for our focus groups. Second, we tried to make people comfortable in the focus groups by using facilitators whose language, ethnicity, and other characteristics matched as closely as possible the groups they were leading. In some cases we paired facilitators so that the demographics of the group were represented in the group's leadership. All of the focus groups, even with different participant characteristics, generated similar key issues, so there was a high level of confidence in the findings. The information we generated has since led to the redesign of the AIDS service delivery system in San Francisco.

— *Mike Allison, Director of Consulting Services*
Support Center for Nonprofit Management

2. Maintaining objectivity

It's easy to lose perspective when gathering a lot of information, especially when it is complicated historical or emotional data. You can listen to one person describe a set of events and their story is entirely believable. The next person tells a different story about the same events, and they also are believable—but the stories are totally contradictory. Where is the boundary between perception and reality and, more important, how do you handle this kind of situation?

If I'm lucky and have listened really well I'm able to figure out why such different views of reality exist. I can then describe this for the client in a constructive way. Much of the time, though, I don't have all the information and don't understand what is behind conflicting stories or information. In that case, I simply bring the conflicting information to the client and we work together to sort it out.

The more difficult situation is when I find myself biased toward one set of data, or one perspective over another. When this happens I need to pay attention to my bias and, if I'm not able to manage it, be honest with the client about my position.

And the most difficult situation is when I find myself moved by someone's anger or pain. Understanding the emotions within the client system is helpful information because you then know what their world is like; getting immobilized by or caught up in the emotions makes you unavailable to assist the client. In those situations I find that I need someone outside the client's system to help me process my reactions and get clear on a course of action.

In some situations emotions are strong and a consultant has to proceed carefully. I was helping an organization with a management audit and strategic planning, and we were in the data collection stage. In this organization board members serve for a long period of time, up to twenty years. Some of the board wanted the executive director removed, and there was a lot of innuendo and hearsay. People wouldn't let go of history and old feelings. Whenever I conclude interviews I say, "Please call me back if you think of anything else," and usually people do not call me back. In this case, seven board members called me back one to three times each with additional stories and incidents. It felt almost like someone was planting stories. And the executive director kept threatening to sue. Given the severity of some of the allegations, I probed with each board member what action they had personally taken in response to the allegations. I tried to help the board to at least take partial responsibility for what had happened. It was impossible to determine fully what was fact, so in my report I added a disclaimer that described the limitations of the study. I was careful to frame issues tactfully so everyone would feel they had been heard, and everyone took some responsibility for their part of the situation. For example, the board admitted it hadn't defined performance expectations for the executive director. Now task forces are in place and they're moving ahead on some of the policy and communication issues that need to be addressed.

— Patty Oertel
President, Oertel Group and former
Executive Director, Southern California
Center for Nonprofit Management

3. Discovering improper or illegal behavior, or actions that violate your values or standards

This situation is the primary reason making a commitment to confidentiality is not advisable. If you encounter illegal or unethical practices, you must gather enough information to verify the situation, and then bring the evidence to the attention of the leadership of the organization or group. Situations you may encounter include harassment, fraud, inequitable compensation or hiring practices, or conflict of interest. Be sure to report immediately and accurately exactly what you have heard or seen, and why it is a concern. Don't get caught up in emotion or panic; the organization will need you to keep a level head and help them figure out how to respond.

Consultants frequently encounter situations that may not be illegal or unethical and may well be consistent with the organization's mission, but that challenge your personal values or standards. These situations vary widely for each consultant, ranging from having to work with a group leader who seems punitive in dealings with people, to discovering poor bookkeeping systems. I've learned to listen to my heart and intuition, confront these discomforts early rather than letting them build, seek peer or professional advice if I need information, talk about them with the client, and if no other solution seems workable, to terminate my consulting relationship.

4. Recognizing your limitations

Be clear about your level of competence in data collection so you don't mislead your client and do poor or misleading research. As you begin planning the data collection effort, you may find that the client's goals change or expand beyond what you initially planned in your agreement with the client. If your client needs information that requires statistical validity, such as public opinion on a community issue in order to influence policy, or information that will stand up to the rigors of a cautious and possibly contentious board, you should consider advising the organization to work with someone with a research background. Or if focus groups seem the best way to proceed and you are not trained or experienced in their use, consider bringing in an outside specialist either to design and conduct the sessions or to train or coach you. A local university or research organization is usually a good resource for help with data collection. You have several options for managing the use of additional resources: you can terminate your contract and advise the client to work with someone with more specialized training, you can subcontract a portion of the work to another consultant, or you can advise the organization to hire an additional resource to work with you.

5. Building your technological competence

Increasingly I find myself sharing information with clients and other consultants electronically. They want a report e-mailed, or they want it on diskette. Or I need their mailing list, which may be in a different format than my computer system uses. We end up converting data back and forth. If you are frequently asked to conduct data collection you will need either familiarity with basic technology or good resource people to turn to for help.

Stage 2 Summary

In the gathering and analyzing stage of the consulting process you:

1. Decided what information is needed and how to get it
2. Communicated with various constituencies about the data collection
3. Gathered needed information
4. Summarized and analyzed information
5. Shared information with the organization or group

You and the client now have a clear picture of what is needed in the client system or in their community, and you are ready to help them create plans for bringing about the changes or creating the products they want to create.

In the next section, Stage 3: Planning the Work, you will assist the client in developing a plan to bring about the desired changes to improve their functioning.

STAGE 3: Planning the Work

When you were first invited in to consult with the group, they asked you to help them do something—develop a plan, create a vision for the neighborhood, design a program, train their board, create a new accounting system, develop stronger teamwork, or develop a fund-raising strategy. In Stage 1 you established an agreement for how you would work with them to do this work. In Stage 2 you collected more information so that the work you did would be aligned with their history, current realities, and future opportunities. In Stage 3 you will refine the organization's or group's goals in light of what you learned in Stage 2 and help them decide how they will accomplish these goals.

One of the gifts and curses of Western culture is the penchant for action. We see a problem and we want to fix it. We don't want to stop and analyze, we want to "just do it." That style works when you are operating alone or in a crisis. When a group is involved, multiple cultures are represented, or the "problem" is complex, a more thoughtful analysis and plan for how the issue will be addressed are needed. When more than one individual will carry out plans and mutual commitment is important, an inclusive planning process is needed that will bring people on board with the plan and create unity of action. The purpose of the third stage is to help the client create a plan that describes *what* they want to accomplish and *how* they will accomplish it. An effective planning process and a solid plan for action will move a group a good part of the way toward achieving their goals. It will also align individual actions with the direction the group is moving.

One of the most frequent consulting requests from nonprofits and community groups is for planning—strategic planning, operational planning, business planning, marketing planning, financial planning, fund-raising planning, crisis planning. Stage 3 may be the central part of your consulting project. Each of these specific kinds of planning is unique, includes different steps, and requires different expertise and skills. This section is not intended to be a primer on strategic planning or fund-raising planning. See Appendix A, Resources, on page 163, for resources in some of these areas. Stage 3 is intended to provide general guidelines about the planning stage of the consulting process—guidelines that can be used with many different kinds of consulting projects.

The following examples illustrate the relationship between Stage 2 and Stage 3 in the consulting process:

Kind of project	*Stage 2 and Stage 3 activities*
Program planning	*You are asked to hold focus groups with residents of a neighborhood to determine what their health care needs are, where they generally go for care, whether they have insurance, and the extent to which they are satisfied with their care (Stage 2). The organization then wants you to help them develop plans that will respond to the needs expressed in the focus groups (Stage 3).*
Team building	*An organization has just restructured their staff, eliminating several key positions. They ask you to help them build strong working relationships in the new work teams. You conduct interviews with management and staff and in a series of meetings work through the data generated in the interviews (Stage 2). You then engage the organization in developing plans for strengthening their work teams (Stage 3).*
Technology planning	*You are asked to assist an organization in choosing a computer system. You have done a thorough assessment of their current and future needs and constraints (Stage 2). You will now help them decide specifically what they hope to accomplish with a new computer system, what technology components they need to accomplish their goals, and how they will accomplish the change (Stage 3).*

Kind of project	*Stage 2 and Stage 3 activities*
Facilitation	*You are asked to facilitate an annual board retreat. You interview board members to determine their concerns and hopes for the retreat (Stage 2). You then work with them to define objectives and an agenda for the retreat (Stage 3).*
Strategic planning	*You are asked to assist a collaborative of seven organizations to develop a strategic plan for their joint effort. After getting agreement on the overall planning process, you assist the group in assessing strengths and weaknesses and environmental forces affecting them (Stage 2). You then move into setting a vision and goals for the future (Stage 3).*

There are five steps involved in Stage 3: Planning the Work. Each of these steps will be described in the following section.

1. Structure the planning process

2. Identify key issues

3. Define goals

4. Develop strategies

5. Prepare an implementation plan

Step 1: Structure the Planning Process

Your first task is to decide how you will create your plan. You will need to answer two questions:

- Who needs to be involved, and in what ways?

- What planning schedule will work? (How long do meetings need to be? How many meetings will we need?)

Who needs to be involved, and in what ways?

Planning can be done by a large group that includes everyone in the organization or collaborative, by a representative planning group, or by multiple task forces, committees, or departments in an organization. Consider who needs to participate in the planning activities and in what way, who needs to be informed of the plans, and who needs to approve the plan. A general rule is to involve people when they are needed for a specific purpose, for example, for their expertise, their buy-in, or their approval. Do not involve them more than what will accomplish that purpose. Planning processes often err by having too many people, too few people, or the wrong people.

Figure 6 below illustrates the main advantages and disadvantages of each planning structure. A little creativity will make it possible to use any of the optional structures and minimize their inherent disadvantages. For example, you can combine two approaches effectively by setting goals with the whole group and then delegating strategy development to several subgroups.

Planning Structures   **Figure 6**

	Advantages	**Disadvantages**
Planning with whole group involvement *Planning Group*	1. Everyone feels ownership of plans. 2. No need to bring people up to speed.	1. Cost of everyone's time is high. 2. Scheduling meetings and reaching agreement can prolong the process.
Planning by a representative subgroup *x x x ... Planning Group*	1. Efficient use of time. 2. Planning process moves quickly.	1. Not everyone buys into the plan. 2. Information can be missed that would improve the plan.
Planning through multiple task forces *Task Force, Task Force, Task Force*	1. Builds ownership with many people. 2. Captures people's interests and expertise.	1. It may be difficult to integrate the subparts into a unified, cohesive overall plan. 2. People may only see "one part of the elephant" and miss interconnections between strategies.

What planning schedule will work? How long do meetings need to be? How many meetings are needed?

Once you have decided on your meeting structure you need to establish a planning schedule and invite people to participate. A planning process can be accomplished in as little as two hours, or can take many hours over months or a year, depending on the complexity of the issues being dealt with. Planning meetings can be two to three hours weekly or bimonthly, or can be all-day sessions. The planning process needs to be tailored to the unique needs of your client situation. Figure 7 below shows a sample planning process outline and schedule.

Figure 7	Sample Planning Process		
Steps		**Responsible**	**By When**
1. In meeting number 1 of the planning committee: • Review data collected in assessment. • Identify critical issues/key strategy areas. • Plan development of strategies for task force effort (assignment, timeline, support needed, etc.).		Planning Committee Staff Consultant	8/1
2. Develop strategies/recommendations.		Task Forces Staff Consultant	9/15
3. Compile task force work into first draft of plan.		Consultant Staff	10/1
4. In meeting number 2 of the planning committee: • Review first draft plan. • Decide revisions. • Decide contingency plans needed. • Decide review process.		Planning Team Staff Consultant	10/15
5. Review draft plan with three focus groups. Incorporate suggested changes as appropriate.		Staff Consultant	11/15
6. In meeting number 3 of the planning committee, finalize plan utilizing focus group input.		Planning Team Staff Consultant	12/1
7. Approve plan.		Steering Committee	1/15
8. Implement plan: • Monitor and modify as appropriate (every six months). • Update plan annually.		Organization	Ongoing

A more abbreviated planning process might include two meetings, one that combines Steps 1 and 2 in Figure 7, and the second that covers Step 4. The following Sample Planning Meeting Agenda (**Figure 8**) illustrates how the first two steps in the sample planning process might be combined into a seven-hour meeting.

Whatever planning process you use, be sure to think carefully through all of the steps and communicate them clearly to everyone who needs to know or be involved in the planning.

Sample Planning Meeting Agenda

Figure 8

(Combines Steps 1 and 2 from planning process outlined in Figure 7.)

11:00	Welcome Introductions	Board chair
11:30	Review survey responses • Findings • Conclusions	Consultant or group representatives
(Working lunch)		
1:00	Identify and prioritize critical issues • Small groups study data report. Select the three most critical issues to pursue during the next year. • Small groups report. • Rank order and confirm selection of priority issues.	Small groups
2:30	Establish goals • In a group visioning exercise, identify what the group hopes will be different in two years for each critical issue. • Confirm goals.	
4:00	Develop initial strategy ideas • Small groups break out to develop strategies for each goal area. • Small groups report to large group. • Large group discusses and expands on strategy ideas.	
5:30	Decide next steps in planning process • Distribute a summary of meeting discussion. • Planning committee and consultant further shape strategy ideas into first-draft plan. • Schedule next planning meeting to review first-draft plan.	
6:00	Adjourn	

Step 2: Identify Key Issues

Now that your planning structure is in place you will begin the work of planning. The second step in the planning stage is to identify or review key issues that emerged from the data collection. This step is sometimes done as part of data feedback, which is the last step in Stage 2.

Planning terminology may vary. Different consultants and organizations will prefer different language, possibly including critical issues, key issues, priority issues, challenges, opportunities, needs, or target areas for change. The terminology isn't as important as making sure that everyone understands the language you are using and getting clarity on the most important issues that need to be addressed for the project to succeed.

Typically the organization or group identifies key issues when they first seek the services of a consultant. Data collection will often expand or change the organization's understanding of these key issues. The following examples illustrate typical key issues that need to be addressed in the planning stage:

Kind of project	Possible key issues
Program planning	• In the last fifteen years, the percentage of people in our service area without health insurance increased by 60 percent. • 38 percent of neighborhood residents have no idea what services our agency provides.
Team building	• The majority of staff are unclear about their new job responsibilities. • Internal communications mechanisms worked in the old structure; in our new structure we aren't getting necessary information to people in a timely manner.
Technology planning	• Priority future technology needs are financial reporting and program data storage and retrieval. • 45 percent of staff haven't had prior experience on computers.
Facilitation	• Our central question is whether to pursue merger discussions with another agency. • Four of the fourteen board members attending are new to the board and don't know the history and direction of the organization.

There are several ways that you can engage the client group in deciding what the key issues are. The most important factor to keep in mind is that *it is the client who has to determine the key issues;* your opinions will be helpful to the client, but they are the ones who need to understand and be committed to addressing the key issues. You can share your opinions and point out important information in the data collected, but they need to decide. The most common methods for determining which key issues to focus on include:

- Base the decision on frequency of information in the data collected. The most frequently mentioned concerns or needs will likely be a high priority for the organization or group.

- Start with priority issues identified in the data, ask the group to add items that might have been missed, and then use a group decision-making process such as nominal group technique[5] or some other group decision-making procedure to reach consensus on which are the most important issues to address.

- Base the decision about priority issues on best-practice models or research in a relevant field that indicates which issues have the greatest likelihood of leveraging desired changes.

- Present possible key issues to appropriate experts or decision makers, in cases where one person or a small group will make the final decision, where the key issues have to be aligned with organizational goals or strategy, or where technical expertise is required to make the best decision.

In some cases you will find that the information unearthed in the assessment is symptomatic of other, sometimes more complex, issues. Be prepared to go back to a brief, more focused data gathering process to clarify underlying issues, if necessary.

By the end of Step 2: Identify Key Issues, you will have a list of the key issues that need to be addressed. In Step 3 you will outline the outcomes or goals the organization hopes to achieve.

---

[5] Developed by Andre Delbecq and Andrew Van de Ven in the 1960s, the nominal group technique is a highly structured group decision-making process that involves soliciting ideas from individuals, exploring them as a group, and then ranking the ideas to arrive at a group decision.

Step 3: Define Goals

An old adage says: "Better know where you're going or you may end up somewhere else." The purpose of Step 3 is to clarify what the client hopes to accomplish—what will be different when they are successful. They need to decide where they are going and how they will get there. By now you will likely be holding the reins on a group of people wanting to race to the finish line. People will want to start deciding immediately what they will do to address their issues. They will have a ton of wonderful ideas about action and about solutions to the key issues. Step 3 suggests that you first need to assist the organization in defining the goals or outcomes that they hope to achieve in the future before talking about strategies or actions.

One of the most important things a consultant brings is a process framework for the client to do their work. I once worked with an old nonprofit that grew out of a church mission. They had a two-part mission, to care for people in poverty and to help them achieve self-sufficiency. They needed clear direction to help them sort out priorities and decide development needs. Their mission was too broad and really two missions in one. My role was to help determine what information was needed ahead of time and who to involve, and to design and facilitate a two-day retreat at which we would clarify mission, outcomes, and their primary customers. We had all stakeholders at the retreat—board, staff, church members, representatives of the church, United Way, and people affected by poverty. I had done some homework on best practices and consulted with experts before to understand the key things for the organization to think about. That preparation allowed me to think and listen well. I didn't guide their choices but stimulated their thinking and let them discover for themselves. Because the issues were so compelling, I had to keep reminding myself not to solve the problem but to provide a process for them to solve their problem. We got to the pivotal moment of deciding what would be the focus of their services out of many compelling needs. We got ten nominations. I sent people out for an hour to ponder their choices. Then we got down to three choices. We divided into three groups and worked out scenarios for each option. I kept thinking, "How will we choose? It's not going to happen." I kept asking the groups to go deeper. With a half hour left, the three groups reported. Instead of three separate scenarios they had created a unified scenario with three parts. They were so exhausted they didn't see it. But I saw it and reflected back to the group what they had created. In less than an hour after the retreat we were able to write up a vision statement, mission statement, and five long-term overarching goals, which were affirmed the next morning. They had used their group wisdom to find their vision. The lesson for me as consultant is that one of the most important things we bring is a process for our clients to come to their own conclusions and frameworks. We need to have faith in people that there is wisdom there; our job is bringing it out. I went away feeling something real was created that would make a difference.

— *Gary J. Stern, President*
Gary J. Stern & Associates, Inc.

Many terms mean "what you hope to accomplish," including goals, outcomes, vision, results, success indicators, and objectives. Assist your client in deciding quickly what terminology to use and what it means to them. The important thing is to help the group decide what they hope to accomplish, or what changes they hope will occur as a result of their work.

The following examples illustrate the transition from key issues to goals.

Kind of project	Key issues	Possible Goals
Program planning	• *In the last fifteen years, the number of uninsured has increased by 60 percent.* • *38 percent of neighborhood residents have no idea what services our agency provides.*	1. *80 percent of people in our neighborhood without health insurance will have access to affordable health care by the year 2002.* 2. *85 percent of neighborhood residents will know what services we provide and how to access these services.*
Team building	• *The majority of staff are unclear about their new job responsibilities.* • *Internal communications mechanisms worked in the old structure; in our new structure we aren't getting necessary information to people in a timely manner.*	1. *All staff will understand their job accountabilities and will know how their performance will be measured.* 2. *Two-way communication systems will be in place to ensure that staff have access to information in a timely manner and know where to go with ideas, questions, or concerns.*
Technology planning	• *We need technology for financial reporting and program data storage and retrieval.* • *45 percent of staff haven't had prior experience on computers.*	1. *Obtain computers and software by January 1.* 2. *All staff will be able to accomplish basic computer functions.*
Facilitation	• *Increasing overlap with other agencies in services and audience.* • *Four of the fourteen board members attending are new and unclear about board responsibilities.*	1. *Determine feasibility of a merger with another agency.* 2. *Develop and implement board orientation and training program.*

When helping an organization or group define their goals or outcomes, five factors are important. Goals, or outcome statements, should:

- Address the key issues identified in Step 2

- Be limited in number so the group can manage their attention

- Be doable—be within the power of the group to achieve

- Describe an end result, not an action or activity

- Be concrete and measurable, if at all possible, so the group will know when they have achieved the goals

Working with faith-based groups adds some different dimensions to consulting. Once I was assisting an urban church with planning. They asked me to look at historical and demographic data on how their neighborhood and congregation were changing and to survey members of the congregation to find out their beliefs about their mission and work in the community. Then we had a one-day session to do visioning. They decided they needed to reach out more to the community and other churches. They came to this through looking at their personal beliefs and values. Talking about personal faith and evangelical mission makes it personal. They felt a calling to do certain types of things. We developed priorities, marketing strategies, work plans, and next steps. But what most influenced the choice of priorities was the question, "What are we being called to do, and how does that drive the organiza-tion." Against that they made it concrete—get more information, reorganize our services, have different hours, remodel space. What is interesting about working with faith-based groups is the addition of the spiritual dimension. Churches will do data collection, but they also listen to what God and Scripture are telling the group. They may have an opening prayer by the pastor and pray for guidance during the planning process. And they make leaps of faith. There may be things the data doesn't describe but they focus on them because they think they should do them, and God will provide the means for doing it. In this work it is important that the consultant is comfortable with integrating the group's beliefs, or using faith-based beliefs as criteria for decisions.

— *Terry Donovan*
Independent Consultant

Once the client has defined their outcomes or goals they can move on to Step 4: Develop Strategies.

Step 4: Develop Strategies

The client and consultant now begin to plan how you will bring about desired changes. Goals (Step 3) define *what* you hope to achieve; strategies (Step 4) describe *how* you will achieve it. The relationship between these two elements is described in the following diagram:

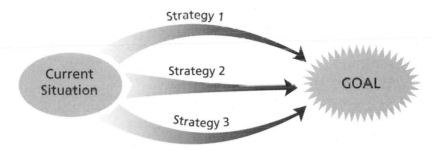

The goals and strategies the client is working on may deal with concrete things such as programs, structure, or organizational systems. They may focus on less concrete areas such as trust, communications, or organizational culture. Or you may jointly, with the client, be designing a short intervention such as a training program or a planning retreat. The client may choose to develop strategies for all of their goals or build strategies for the first phase of the change effort with the intention of implementing those and then developing strategies for the next phase of work. In all of these cases, the process of identifying and formulating alternative paths of action toward the goal is one of the most creative—and sometimes most difficult—challenges for the consultant and the client.

The process of developing strategies or interventions generally includes the following substeps:

1. Brainstorm alternative strategies or designs for how they will achieve their goal. You may need to obtain expert input if you are working in a new area. Worksheet 1: Developing Goals and Strategies in Appendix C, Client Worksheets, on page 187, can be used in this activity.

2. Clarify criteria that will be used to select strategies (for example, strategies must fit with our mission and values, strengthen or enhance our current programs, be acceptable to a majority of our board and staff, and be fundable.) See Worksheet 2: Ranking Strategies on page 189 in Appendix C.

3. Weigh alternative strategies against your criteria. Some will fit better than others. Select the most promising strategies.

4. Explore the risks, consequences, and potential side effects of the strategies you have chosen. If needed, revamp your strategies or build in contingency plans to fall back on if strategies are not successful.

Sometimes a client isn't ready to act, at least in a way the consultant thinks they should. I just completed a most challenging board retreat for a student organization. One of their long-standing funders wanted them to develop a strategic plan. The organization agreed to the strategic plan and a fund-raising plan, mostly to be polite to the funder. But the organization didn't feel any pressing need for it. They are perfectly content to grow incrementally, and to keep their board fairly informal. They have a number of issues, and they don't have a high need to get closure on any of them. The board operates with no committees, and they have the same repetitive discussion at board meetings. The participants were drinking and spilling wine during the retreat, and in the middle of the session, the group took a break to watch themselves on TV. In spite of their looseness, they are achieving a strong measure of success. No one seemed frustrated but me. I have a need for closure on issues, but I didn't feel it was appropriate for me to put my need for closure on the group. They finally agreed to address some of the issues and decide on action steps, and were thrilled by the end of the session. With groups that are indecisive, unfocused, or reluctant to make decisions, I've learned to use some techniques like circular decision making—make one decision and then make a second decision, and then test whether the second decision indicates that the first decision needs to be changed. This helps groups move. But I have to distinguish between what I am pushing and what they need and want. I can raise issues, but if the group isn't ready to embrace them, it's not for me to push. Until the client feels a pressing need, they probably won't take action.

— *Patty Oertel*
President, Oertel Group and former
Executive Director, Southern California
Center for Nonprofit Management

There are several principles to keep in mind as you assist the client in developing strategies—sequence, system level, participation, timing and momentum, and quality. These are described in the following sections.

Sequence

The sequence of strategies or interventions is an important decision when developing the plan. In some cases the sequence will be obvious; in others the sequence becomes a crucial design factor that can significantly influence success. Some rules of thumb to keep in mind include:

- *Form follows function.* Generally consider system-wide changes before addressing the specifics. If there are questions about mission, goals, or strategy they should be addressed before addressing structural or operational issues.

- *Make a hallmark change or decision early.* Highly visible, symbolic changes early in the process will create confidence and generate commitment. For example, a new president of a large, established, hierarchical organization threw away the "president only" sign on the best spot in the parking lot. This symbolized a dramatic change in leadership style and culture for the organization.

- *Move with the energy in the organization.* Sometimes there is great energy to work on one particular thing, even though in many ways it isn't the logical place to start. Success in one area that is meaningful to people can generate enthusiasm to work in other areas.

- *Attend to the developmental stage* of the organization or group. For example, a newly forming group of people or collaboration of organizations needs time to learn about each other and work through issues of leadership and influence before working well as a team. A large, established organization may need to initiate changes slowly in order to bring all parts of the organization on board.

- *Phase in changes.* Change can sometimes be overwhelming for people. It may be helpful to define phases of the work, so even though people know there are a number of areas to work on, only two will be addressed during the next six months.

- *Balance urgency with importance.* Some goals need immediate attention for short-term health or survival; others are crucial to long-term success. Both need to be addressed.

System level

Where to intervene or begin changes is important to consider. When I refer to the term *system* I mean an entity or network that has interconnected and interdependent subparts. Changes in one subpart affect other subparts of a system, and therefore cause alterations in the larger system. Six possible system levels need to be considered in planning interventions[6]:

- *Intrapersonal level:* Factors involving one person and their attitudes, values, skills, knowledge, and behavior.

- *Interpersonal level:* Factors in the dynamics between two people, such as their roles, work assignments, or communications.

- *Group level:* Factors affecting the performance of more than two people who are engaged in a common task. This might include a work team, a committee, or a board.

- *Intergroup level:* Factors affecting the relationship between two groups, such as two departments in an organization, two neighborhoods, two committees of the board, or the board and staff of an organization.

- *Organization-wide level:* Factors affecting multiple groups or parts of an organization.

- *Community level:* Factors affecting the broader community or industry, which has many interrelated organizations or units.

---

[6] Robert Blake and Jane Mouton, in their book *Consultation* (Reading, Mass.: Addison-Wesley, 1976, page 6), identify five system levels: individual, group, intergroup, organization, and larger social systems. The authors provide in-depth guidance on intervention within each level.

As a general rule, intervention is most effective at the level where the *underlying* issue exists, which is not necessarily how the presenting problem is identified or where the pain is felt. Usually this is at least one level broader than where the identified issue is located because this is where the leverage exists to resolve the issue. Careful diagnosis is needed to determine this. For example, if there is recurrent conflict between two groups (work units, committees), it may be an intergroup conflict that can be resolved by those two groups; it may exist because the broad goals of those groups are not clear and need to be clarified at a higher level in the organization or community; or it may be because of a lack of skills in communications and conflict resolution at the individual level with people in the groups. An intervention in any one part of a system will have impact throughout the system. Watch for influences from and repercussions on the whole organization or community you are working with.

Participation

Who to involve, when, and how to involve them are important questions to resolve in your planning. Some general guidelines about involvement and participation include:

- *Avoid token participation.* Be clear about the reason for involving people. Let them know whether they are being invited to give input or feedback, to develop recommendations, to make decisions, to endorse a decision that's been made, or to be influenced or convinced about something. Make sure people are involved from the beginning who have the technical expertise needed to do the work well.

- *Build ownership.* Those most affected by decisions need to be integrally involved in making the decision. If you want people to be committed to something, the degree of their commitment or feeling of ownership will be directly related to both their involvement in the decision making and their accountability for bringing about change.[7] The relationship between ownership, involvement, and accountability can be shown as follows:

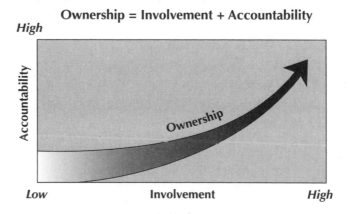

Ownership = Involvement + Accountability

---

[7] Mike Allison, Support Center for Nonprofit Management of San Francisco, helped clarify this concept.

- *Structure representation.* To get widespread commitment from a large organization, system, or broad community, involve representatives from throughout the system to work on the change effort. This can be done by inviting people to volunteer to work where their interests lie, by having a representative group that includes all subparts of the organization, collaborative, or neighborhood, or by having a smaller group delegated to do the work with adequate review sessions with the larger audience. The use of task forces to focus on discrete areas of planning is an effective way to involve many people. Worksheet 3: Task Force Planning, in Appendix C, Client Worksheets, on page 191, can be used when planning with task forces.

- *Provide choices.* People generally want choice in how they participate. If possible, provide options for people rather than expecting participants to conform to a fixed schedule or one-time event.

- *Ensure diversity.* The mantra for nonprofits and community groups is "who's not at the table who should be?"[8] As our communities and organizations become more diverse, the composition at the decision-making table needs to become more diverse. Unfortunately, the representation at the decision-making table rarely mirrors the communities we serve, and extra effort is needed to make sure that the real stakeholders of our efforts are involved in decision making.

- *Involve stakeholders.* Organizations and even neighborhoods can no longer afford to be insular in their thinking or actions. For almost any decision that needs to be made, or any change effort, there are valuable resources, policymakers, colleagues, constituents, and potential sponsors or funders outside the group, organization, or community who can potentially add value to your effort. Be creative in finding ways to keep all stakeholders on board and contributing.

Timing and momentum

How long does it take to bring about change? How fast can people, organizations, or communities change? Normally changes take a great deal of time to be communicated, to gain support, and to be completed. For example, a change in the structure of an organization, although decided quickly, can take one to two years to be fully implemented and internalized by all members of the organization. Some general guidelines for timing and momentum follow.

- *Maintain momentum.* Sequence strategies so that sufficient time is allowed to do a thorough job of implementation, but with a balance of long-term strategies and short-term visible actions that will keep people's energy focused on the outcomes. Build in review times so that people know what has been accomplished and what the next steps are.

---

[8] Minneapolis-based consultant Michael Groh started challenging the author about inclusion in planning meetings in the early 1980s.

- *Keep the plan elastic.* Conditions will change, crises will occur, things will take longer than expected, staff will turn over, and visions may expand. Build in some flexibility in timing, along with periodic reviews, to adjust for changing conditions.

Usually clients are ripe for getting closure, and we can make decisions without much difficulty. In one case, my clients had a difficult time choosing a direction. I was assisting a school for youth with special needs to develop a strategic plan. It was intended to be a four to six month planning process, and it actually took eighteen months. The group had an exceedingly high need for process. They wouldn't let go of any option unless it was fully explored and discussed. I had to renegotiate the contract three times, including fee increases. I had to keep finding different tools and techniques to help them weigh options and narrow their focus. After we finally went through a thorough analysis, it ended up that all their choices were roughly equal. We had to find a way to test options. So we set up a plan to go with one option, define a measure of success for it, monitor whether it was working, and then based on their experience with that option, modify what they were doing or move on to a second option. We left all of the options in the plan so they didn't have to give up any.

— *Patty Oertel*
President, Oertel Group and former
Executive Director, Southern California
Center for Nonprofit Management

Quality

One of the most important questions is whether your client has developed strategies that are good ones. Are they likely to achieve the desired results? You may not have the expertise in your client's field to know whether the strategies will work. If you don't, challenge the client to test their likelihood of success.

- *Make sure strategies and choices are aligned with mission and values.* The most artful strategy can result in serious problems if it is not consistent with the mission and values of the organization.

- *Borrow from research or best practice models.* Do your homework and assist the client in doing theirs. A lot of information is available, whatever the field you are working in, about what works and doesn't work in different situations. Make sure that plans or decisions are technically sound. If you are facilitating a process and relying on the group's expertise, test the need for outside expertise.

- *Test through pilot projects.* Pilot projects are useful for testing an untried strategy, or as the first phase in a complex plan to get support from people throughout the system.

- *Assess impact and risk.* For each strategy you have identified, assist the client in identifying the direct and indirect impact that the strategy is likely to have, and the areas of greatest risk or vulnerability it poses. Where necessary, develop contingency plans or revise strategies as needed to strengthen the overall plan.

One organization taught me that the difference between an adequate plan and a great plan is often a matter of heart. A maternal and infant care program, which had been quite successful in improving the health and prospects of at-risk mothers and newborns, asked for help in developing a strategic plan. The staff's extraordinary commitment to the well-being of young moms and their babies, plus their flexible and inventive style, were primary reasons for the organization's success. Early in the planning we determined that over half of the program's funding would be lost over the next twelve months due to government budget cuts. The program's survival was at stake. A core planning group worked very hard to find a way to continue providing these important services in a manner which could be sustained financially. After much hard work, we discovered a way to solve the tough financial problems, and drafted a strategic plan. It seemed like a good plan. In reviewing the draft with staff, I noticed several sad faces. I mentioned possible reasons for this reaction, such as staff reductions, and asked, "Why the long faces?" The spiritual rock of the group noted, "When I consider how we plan to structure and operate our program in the future, I'm not sure that this will be the kind of organization where I want to work. I fear that we will squeeze the flexibility out of our program, which has been the key to our success. But I don't see another alternative." Others nodded in agreement.

The group decided to form three teams to continue exploring how the program could be sustained financially *and* serve moms and children in the manner required. One team came back with a great approach which was adopted, and the organization was able to thrive. I often think of this lesson— planning fully with both your head and heart. I now check periodically with the groups I serve, to see if both head and heart are well-engaged. It's a key to great planning and organizational success.

— *Bryan Barry*
Amherst H. Wilder Foundation

In Step 4 you developed strategies to help the client reach their desired goals. In Step 5 you will create an implementation plan that will lay out action steps that need to be taken to accomplish the goals.

Step 5: Prepare an Implementation Plan

An implementation plan is crucial for ensuring that the goals and strategies identified will actually be implemented, and for getting all stakeholders pulling in the same direction toward achievement of the goals. The implementation plan also provides a concrete way to involve the board and ensure their support of the change effort. In addition, an implementation plan:

- Clarifies specific steps that need to be taken
- Designates who will be responsible for accomplishing each step
- Establishes a timeline for implementation
- Provides a means of keeping momentum going and of monitoring progress

- Ensures that communications will be maintained throughout the process

- Outlines resources needed and how resources will be obtained

Typical sections of an implementation plan are:

- *Background*: Includes events and circumstances leading to the development of the plan.

- *Goals and strategies*: Defines specific outcomes to be achieved and strategies describing how they will be accomplished.

- *Action plan*: Outlines steps needed to accomplish each goal or strategy, who is responsible for each step, time frame, and target dates.

- *Communications*: Outlines how people both inside and outside the organization or group will be kept informed and involved in the process; explains how input from people will be obtained.

- *Resources*: Describes a range of resources needed including leadership, people, expertise, money; and explains how these resources will be obtained.

- *Monitoring*: Defines how progress on implementation will be monitored and how the plan will be refined as needed.

An implementation plan helps to ensure that everyone involved in the change effort is on the same page and pulling together to achieve the goals.

Worksheet 4: Implementation Plan, will help you prepare an implementation plan. It is included in Appendix C, Client Worksheets, on page 193.

Challenges in Stage 3

1. Getting people on board

Some people don't like change, while others are impatient with planning. Others believe that "the way we've always done things has worked fine and shouldn't be tinkered with." And most people involved with nonprofits (in either a staff or volunteer capacity) or working in the community are already stretched thin with demands and overloaded schedules. The challenge is to make the planning process exciting, relevant, and creative so that people will be energized by their participation.

If I were to identify the three things that will have the greatest impact on the success of a planning process, they would be (1) to establish effective decision-making procedures so good decisions are made with respect for people's time; (2) to use a process that builds relationships between people and generates energy; and (3) to have doable plans.

2. Planning for the future is not a familiar concept or practice in all cultures

Many cultures do not use planning as the way to get from here to there. They may be more present- or action-oriented, or simply not have experience thinking about the future and creating a concrete plan to guide their way. Planning is also rife with jargon—mission, vision, positioning, goals, outcomes, niche, alignment, objectives, strategies, tactics, steps, interventions, SWOT analysis[9], gap analysis—the list goes on. Even a group of people who have similar cultural characteristics will rarely agree on the definition of some of these terms.

It seems that the more diverse our audiences are, the more organic the process has to be, and the less you can predict what will happen. For example, a highly diverse group of writers met to fill an unmet need for a community-based organization where writers' courses would occur at restaurants, coffeehouses, or theaters, and which would attract other diverse writers. The group of writers included whites, blacks, Asian Americans, Latinos, and Native Americans. They brought me in to help with their strategic planning. Part way through the planning process, we started doing visioning. After several hours, we realized we weren't going anywhere. It seems each person had a very different concept of visioning. We had each person in the group describe what they thought strategic planning was and why it was important. Quite a few different images of strategic planning emerged. What we chose was an organic and powerful way to proceed, called *self-organizing systems*, where you define what your values are, reflect on how to implement those values, and keep talking. Gradually, the system emerges that is needed to implement those values. It worked very well. We ended up with a strategic plan useful for linear thinkers, which also met the need of more organic, less linear thinkers. What I'm talking about is not going to be that unusual in a few years; organization development and management development are moving toward this, incorporating chaos theory and other more diverse ways of thinking into a new paradigm for organizations. It's hard to prepare a consulting contract for this. A standard linear consulting contract defines the outcome, the objectives, the work plan, and the deliverables to show us we're on track. But in highly diverse groups, the process changes frequently. This was confusing and frustrating for me during the project, but by the end, it was probably the best consulting I had ever done—the project where I learned the most.

— *Carter McNamara*
Independent Consultant, formerly with MAP for Nonprofits, which matches volunteers from the for-profit sector with nonprofits needing consulting assistance

Let the group or organization you are working with be your guide. They brought in a consultant to help them accomplish something, so they have an end result in mind. And they've had experience going through changes, whether in their personal or work lives. Help them to draw from their past experience to state what has worked well in bringing about change. If they are part of an immigrant culture, ask when they left their country what they did first, what steps were most helpful in their preparations, what they did when obstacles arose in execution of their journey. If your client

---

[9] SWOT analysis (strengths, weaknesses, opportunities, threats) is a common step in strategic planning.

typically works in a crisis style with little long-term thinking or planning, ask them how that style works for them, if there are times when it doesn't work, how they would like to operate differently, or what the steps were to bring about their greatest accomplishment in the last two years.

> People have become cynical about ordinary consulting work and meetings, flip charts, agendas. I'm using more organic approaches rather than what I think of as traditional consulting. I try to revive a sense of ritual purpose about coming together. I have begun to allow for a sense of prayerfulness at the beginning of forums and meetings to acknowledge and honor the process, to say "We believe the process will work and will try it with an open mind. We recognize that we are about to work hard together to achieve something. There are powers bigger than us at work. We will have a good meeting." Some consultants I know will burn sage and have a formal blessing at the beginning and at the end of a meeting. For many of us, it is necessary to recognize the natural world and the spirit of our ancestors in making our decisions.
>
> — *Ruth Yellow Hawk*
> *Independent Consultant*

3. Balancing depth and pace

It can be a challenge to maintain a balance between enough discussion and analysis to result in a good plan and keeping momentum so the process doesn't get bogged down and you lose people. I find that addressing this question early—when you develop the design for the planning process—will help you find the right balance and establish clear expectations among members for both depth and pace.

4. Watching overuse of pet solutions

It's tempting to keep using or recommending the same strategies or approaches that have worked in the past. However, every client situation is unique and strategies need to be tailored to fit their situation. The biggest advantage to working in a team of consultants—or to having a strong network of consultants that you confer with—is in the new ideas and approaches that you learn. Keep expanding your repertoire through reading, talking to other consultants, and participating in development activities. The bottom line is that the goals and strategies are your client's, and the client has to understand them and own them.

Stage 3 Summary

In the third stage of the consulting process you helped your client decide what they hope to accomplish and how they will accomplish it. The client and others who will be involved in or affected by the effort have outlined goals, strategies, and a timeline for accomplishing the project goals. Your client knows where they are going and how they will get there. Although it may seem as if the journey is just beginning, they have really been on the road all along. By this time significant change is likely to have happened in the client system. They have better information about their situation and clearer focus on their future direction. They have now reached a very exciting stage, which involves activating the plans that have been created.

STAGE 4: Implementing and Monitoring

In Stages 1 through 3 you developed a relationship with the client and scoped out the work to be done; gathered necessary information to inform plans and decisions; and developed a plan for what you wanted to achieve and how you would achieve it. The implementation and monitoring stage is when plans developed in Stage 3 are carried out, and progress monitored to make sure that efforts are having the desired impact.

In some cases the consultant is involved in implementation to a limited extent. For example, a fund-raising, strategic planning, or neighborhood planning consultant may terminate the consulting relationship when the plan is completed. Or, the consultant's involvement with the client may be limited to specific aspects of implementation or to periodic review and updating of their plan.

In other cases implementation may be the main event. For example, if the consulting project focuses on restructuring within an organization, the plan might describe the goals to be achieved and the structure that will be created. The implementation stage involves the actual changeover to a new structure, including all of the program or staffing changes, role negotiations, system changes, and communications needed to support that effort.

You, the consultant, might coach the executive director throughout the change process. You might help to train staff in new job responsibilities. You might advise on changes in financial reporting systems. You might do team development with new work teams. You might help them to monitor the change monthly, to make sure they're addressing any glitches that might occur.

The steps or activities included in the implementation stage, and the consultant role, are unique to the type of consulting you do and the nature of the plans developed by your client. Figure 9 shows examples of the relationship between goals, implementation strategies, and the consultant's roles.

Figure 9 | **Examples of Implementation Strategies and Consultant Roles**

If your goals and plans focus on . . .	Implementation strategies might include . . .	And the consultant role might be . . .
Board development	• board training • policy development • revision of bylaws	• trainer • advisor • referral to attorney
Strengthening teamwork	• role clarification • skill development • changing meeting norms • assignment of team leaders	• facilitator • trainer • coach/facilitator • advisor
Strategic changes	• program development • staff expansion • restructuring • joint venture exploration	• not involved • not involved • advisor • facilitator
Workforce development	• meetings with other providers • setting up computer system with job links	• facilitator • referral to specialist
Adding child care services	• expansion of space • staff changes • promotional campaign	• not involved • not involved • referral to marketing specialists
Attracting new businesses to a neighborhood	• development of a neighborhood video • media campaign • meetings with potential new business owners	• not involved • not involved • facilitator

Specific implementation steps will vary with each project. However, there are three steps to keep in mind during implementation. Even if you won't be directly involved in implementation, you can make these suggestions to the client and build them into the implementation plan. The three steps are:

1. Complete implementation activities

2. Attend to communication and participation

3. Monitor and make adjustments throughout the system

Step 1: Complete Implementation Activities

Finally you can put into place the changes you've planned—whether it's starting a new service, installing a new bookkeeping system, launching a board training program, or even holding a staff planning retreat. The careful assessment and planning you've done will pay off during implementation.

As the client begins implementing plans or changes, you can coach them in two areas:

1. *Delegation*: Usually many people are involved in implementation. They need clear assignments and definitions of their authority and accountability.

2. *Coordinating mechanism*: If changes are being implemented in several areas, the client needs a way to make sure these parallel efforts are working in tandem.

Other implementation needs will be unique to the type of project you are working on. Your level of involvement in the implementation will vary, but this is the client's main event. The best service you can offer your client is to support them, help solve the inevitable glitches that occur, and help them anticipate ways to improve their efforts.

Step 2: Attend to Communication and Participation

The client's task is to bring about the changes they have carefully planned, but how they do this—the process they use—is critical to success. The process is as important as the product. The following process hints will help you keep the process healthy and productive:

Get everyone on board

The last step in Stage 3, Planning the Work, was to develop an implementation plan. Before beginning implementation, make sure that everyone either involved in the change or affected by it understands what you're trying to accomplish, what overall strategies will be used, specific responsibilities of each person, and how new ideas or problems can be addressed during implementation. A good implementation plan will specifically address questions of what, how, who, when, and why. Each person affected by the change should be able to answer those questions in relation to their own job, so that they feel part of the change and so that all individuals and parts of the system are pulling together to make it happen.

Maintain momentum

This is what folks have been waiting for—finally they will carry out plans that have been set. There's likely to be a lot of excitement as well as some trepidation. Most people find that things never go exactly as planned, they always take longer than expected, and there's always someone who seems to be putting their foot on the brake—trying to stop or stall the process.

To keep momentum, it's often useful to assign overall responsibility for implementation to one central person or an implementation team. The lead (person or team) doesn't necessarily need to know the specifics about changes in all of the subareas, but their job is to make sure the process is moving along, and that problems that may arise are dealt with. They become the champion for the change effort. The lead person or team can manage communications, schedule meetings, and do anything else needed to make sure everyone's heading in the same direction as the implementation moves forward.

Communicate!

Both internal and external communications serve several purposes. First, they keep the overall goals of the project in front of people, inspiring them toward the end result, instead of getting bogged down in the day-to-day work. Second, communication mechanisms are needed to keep people informed of progress and changes to plans or strategies. Communication channels also need to be established in many directions: among people working on changes, from the leadership to the group, and from people in the trenches to the central or lead person. Regular meetings to monitor progress and troubleshoot any problems that have emerged are useful during this time.

Times of change are ripe for rumors and misinformation. Since nature abhors a vacuum, if there is inadequate "official" information about what is happening, the rumor mill will tend to kick in and fill the vacuum. So a diligent communication effort stifles rumors and keeps people on board with changes.

Support individuals

In Stage 3, we talked about levels of systems involved in the project or changes. It's often easier to pay attention to the broader levels (such as group, organizations, or community) and more difficult to think about the kind of support the individual employees, stakeholders, managers, or residents might need. Information meetings, training sessions, and opportunities for meaningful involvement are all important to keep people engaged and prepare them for participating in whatever changes are happening. Equally important is finding ways to acknowledge and reward individual achievement or effort.

For example, let's say a community health center is in the process of creating a new program to address the needs of the growing population of elderly in the neighborhood. Most of the implementation energy goes into program planning, hiring staff, obtaining space, developing promotional materials, and so forth. Meanwhile, the employees in the rest of the organization working in their old jobs aren't directly involved in these changes. But once the new program is up and running, employees from throughout the organization will need to understand the nature of the service, the kind of needs it will address in the community, and how to make appropriate referrals between programs. Since they're a major contact point with the public and will have a role in making the new program successful, this is the time to start educating them about the new program and developing referral mechanisms between the traditional medical services and the new elderly program. This agency might even consider a "dry run" with several people pretending to be potential clients and moving through the various stops for information and referral in order for staff to learn how to help new clients successfully.

Step 3: Monitor and Make Adjustments throughout the System

Changes will rarely occur as you have planned them. Conditions change, you get new unexpected information, funding falls short, you get a brilliant idea about how to improve on the plan, or a key staff person leaves. Remember that change is a process and that the most important thing is to help the client set up a mechanism to constantly monitor progress and change their approach as needed. The feedback mechanisms will tell whether changes are happening as planned, if unforeseen circumstances are occurring that need attention, and whether people—program participants, staff, community members—are on board with the changes. Several common ways that organizations do this are:

- Schedule formal review times, such as monthly or quarterly, to check progress and deal with challenges or opportunities that may arise.

- Assign a lead person or implementation team to be the point on the project; let everyone in the organization or group know that the lead person or team is where they can get information or raise concerns.

- If the consultant hasn't been involved in implementation, scheduling a progress review time with the consultant can help the organization check progress and get assistance on persistent challenges.

- If project costs have been funded by an outside source, making a periodic progress report to the funder forces an assessment of progress for the organization.

Whatever method of monitoring progress is used, it is crucial to observe progress on changed plans, make adjustments as needed, and find or create opportunities for celebration. Changes take their toll on everyone; celebrations and rituals can be important to acknowledge and reward effort and results.

Whether or not you are directly involved in the implementation stage with your client, these three steps will help your client manage their implementation process and achieve the results they set out to accomplish.

Challenges in Stage 4

1. Being aware of your own cultural filters

During the implementation stage you will likely have more of a background role, coaching and assisting the client when needed, and observing their progress. The value you add as an outsider is in observing and naming areas that may need attention or that may pose problems in the future. Decisions the client makes during implementation may not always fit with your concept of the "right" way to do things. Whether you agree or not is not the issue. Or your relationship may become strained because of different styles and interaction patterns. The question is whether their chosen path will work for them and get the results they desire.

The critical issue for my consulting in Australia has been learning enough about their culture so I don't impose my own cultural assumptions. Australia is modern, English speaking, and in many ways similar to our culture. The cultural differences are subtle, and you don't know in advance where the differences are and how to alter your approach to fit their ways. Nonprofit management as a specialized field has low awareness. I was working with a church-based human service organization in Melbourne. It's an old organization attached to a very old church. They were technically a freestanding organization, but the church held close reins on the organization. I was engaged by the executive and their management council (board of directors) to do board development. I studied their documentation, board minutes, and information on each board member. I also learned what I could about language issues, assumptions about the structure, and rules about how you got appointed to the board. I modified my normal board development curriculum. I introduced the whole process carefully. I prepared a glossary at the beginning, then made a commitment that I would use their terminology but if I slipped they would know what I was talking about. I gave them permission to challenge my assumptions and ideas. I slowed the process down. I didn't just tell what best practice was. I put some ideas out and then invited dialogue about what fit. I've learned that when working across cultures to ground myself thoroughly; not to position myself as having "the answer" that they should adopt; to build in more time; and to become aware of my own cultural assumptions and experience.

— *Carol L. Barbeito, Ph.D., President*
Applied Research and Development
Institute International

Different cultures handle conflict differently. I was working closely with one person in a Southeast Asian social service agency as I helped them develop a strategic plan. We worked well together and got to know each other well. However, in a few meetings and during a planning retreat I challenged some of his suggestions, mostly to clarify them for myself and the rest of the group. I didn't pay much attention to this initially. Midway through the retreat I noticed that he seemed to be avoiding me and acting distant and sullen. He left the meeting early and somewhat abruptly. I wanted to have a sit down, face-to-face discussion with him after the retreat but he didn't return my calls. Just as I was thinking about calling his boss for help, I ran into him at a banquet to honor a retiring community leader. We made eye contact and smiled. A little later I went over to say hello to him. We shook hands and he introduced me to his friends as his "friend" and "a very important consultant." After that it felt normal again between us. He called me a couple days later with some work-related questions. I asked him what had happened. There was a long pause, then he said, "I thought you were my friend but in our meetings you don't act like my friend. When you disagree with me, I look bad in front of the board and then I got mad. When you came over to me at the banquet I knew you were still my friend, so it's okay now." That was it. The conflict was resolved in his mind. We didn't need to discuss it any further. I've learned that talking about the conflict or "putting your baggage on the table" is only one way of resolving conflicts. Sometimes talking about the conflict can exacerbate it. It may help to wait it out instead of trying to analyze it. For many Southeast Asians, avoiding the conflict or accommodating to another's wishes may be preferable because it's easier, it helps to preserve harmony in the relationship, and it prevents "loss of face" for all involved.

— *Vijit Ramchandani*
Amherst H. Wilder Foundation

Some cultures don't say "no" directly. I was working with a refugee organization, trying to get the board to respond to a serious financial problem. I was pushing them to make a decision. What I didn't know was that this particular group would not say no directly, but would say it in other ways. I asked to be on the agenda of a board meeting, and was scheduled for 7:30. At 7:30 I stuck my head in the door and was told to sit outside till they were done; they would call me when they were ready. After an hour I stuck my head in again and they said, "So sorry we have taken so much time, can you wait a little longer? We know what you have to talk about is very important." At 9:30 I went in and said it is late, maybe we can do it at another time. They responded, "Yes, it is so unfortunate, we'll do it at the next board meeting." I went outside. Something made me sit in my car on the street. Within ten minutes, the place emptied and everyone went home. They didn't want to tell me directly, but were telling me indirectly that they didn't want to deal with the finance issue. I realized my pushing wasn't going to get a decision. I met with the executive director and asked how we should proceed. He said it was necessary for him to meet with the board alone. He needed the board to see him in control of the budget situation. If the consultant takes too strong of a role, it reflects on the director. I had to work through him and not be present when he met with the board. Several months later the organization had to meet with their funders, and they wanted me to do the presentation. They knew that my presence would lend legitimacy in the mainstream culture. I've learned that you need to be aware of indirect communications and also attend to how power is manifested in different cultures.

— *Name withheld at consultant's request*

2. People saying they don't need follow-up help, but really they do

Most community groups and nonprofits have limited budgets for consulting. Often, they underestimate the work they need help with, the amount of time they need, and the amount of follow-up support that will be helpful. In the contracting stage they want to invest all of the money in the up-front planning and feel they can handle it on their own from that point. And in many cases this is true.

However, in over fifteen years of evaluating consulting projects, I've found that a significant number of clients have said they could have used more follow-up support. They would have liked to have the consultant stay with them for three or six months to keep them on track and make adjustments as they proceeded. This is in hindsight, of course. So, as consultants, how do we help the client understand how useful it is to have an outside person supporting them during implementation?

I usually suggest during the contracting stage that we build in some time for implementation or follow-up. If the client resists, I'll usually let it go but then raise it again when writing the implementation plan.

I might ask if having someone available to facilitate check-in meetings or to provide support and coaching to people involved in implementing changes might be helpful. If a client still isn't interested, I'll usually let them know that if they need any kind of additional support, they can always call me, and I will be available to come work with them.

3. Facing the temptation to do it yourself

The secondary goal of consulting (as we mentioned earlier) is to help the client develop the skills and capacity to do it themselves the next time. Just like a parent with a teenager, the consultant often finds it tempting to "do it yourself" rather than to take the time to train, coach, and explain how the client can do it. It's difficult to watch them make "unnecessary" mistakes. But coaching, mentoring, teaching, and watching the client make some mistakes as they try out new behaviors or new skills are necessary to achieve the secondary goal of helping to build the client's capacity for the future.

4. Recontracting

As we mentioned, nothing ever goes quite as planned. The work plan and budget you so carefully developed and negotiated in Stage 1: Contracting, has likely been stretched, changed, and ignored during the course of the consulting project. As you move into implementation, you will very likely need to recontract for unexpected roles or support that the client needs. Don't hesitate to pull out the original contract, review it with the client, and determine whether changes are needed in objectives, tasks, or budget.

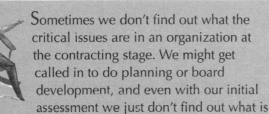

Sometimes we don't find out what the critical issues are in an organization at the contracting stage. We might get called in to do planning or board development, and even with our initial assessment we just don't find out what is really going on, what the root problems are, until we are in the organization for a while. In one case we started to do board training. As we did that we discovered that the client was in financial crisis with deep cash flow problems. The director, who was a founder of the organization, was overcontrolling and not bringing information to the board. An approach we've found to be very useful is to form a crisis management team made up of an officer, the chair or treasurer, and a reliable staff member. We take a heavy facilitating role and provide strong direction to help the crisis management team identify problems and figure out what to do to stop the short-term problem so it doesn't cripple the organization. Once a plan for addressing the immediate issues is in place, the organization can proceed to work on longer-term development efforts. We've learned not to do board development or strategic planning when organizations are in a crisis, unless these tasks are part of resolving the crisis.

— *Larry Guillot, Executive Director*
Center for Management Assistance

Stage 4 Summary

Stage 4: Implementation and Monitoring is often viewed as the feature presentation, the work that the client set out to do from the beginning. Your client has implemented (successfully, of course) all the plans that were so carefully laid out. They have accomplished what they set out to do.

But they—and you—are not finished with the project if you want to accomplish the twin goals of consultation to help the client accomplish their goals *and* to build their capacity to handle similar issues in the future. You have two more stages to complete. These stages are much shorter than the first four but are important to helping the client build their capacity and to successfully concluding your consulting project.

Stage 5: Sustaining Change and Evaluating Impact will help the client understand the impact that their plans have had and will help the client make sure that the plans or changes that they've executed will continue successfully in the future.

STAGE 5: Sustaining Change and Evaluating Impact

The purpose of the fifth stage is for the client to determine the extent to which the plans or changes they've implemented have had the intended impact and are likely to continue into the future. The client will also want to celebrate progress and successes that have been accomplished.

This stage is easy to ignore. The excitement of planning and the challenges of implementation are over and you and the client are probably ready to move on. It's easy for the client to slip back into the old ways of doing things, or even put the new plan on the shelf and go back to business as usual. It is also easy to get distracted by urgent matters that arise day by day and not continue new efforts or changes that were created.

The following four steps will guide your client in making sure that changes are sustained and progress or accomplishments are acknowledged.

1. Review progress or results in achieving goals

2. Make changes or adjustments as needed

3. Set up an ongoing monitoring process

4. Celebrate progress and success

Step 1: Review Progress or Results in Achieving Goals

In reviewing progress toward accomplishing the client's goals, there are two main questions to answer: Have the changes that they have created been integrated with other parts of the organization's operations? and Have the project's goals been accomplished?

Have the changes that they have created been integrated with other parts of the organization's operations?

Your consulting project may have involved adding new services or programs in an organization. During implementation the structure was changed as planned. The question now is whether all of the loose ends surrounding those structure changes have been addressed. If a new program was created, do other people in the organization understand what that program is doing and are they able to communicate to the public about that program? Has the accounting system been adjusted to serve the new financial needs of the program? Has the organization hired and trained staff adequately to handle the volume of work that's generated?

A different kind of project might have focused on training board members to serve in a different kind of governing role. All board members have received training, new expectations have been negotiated between the board and the executive director, and board meetings seem to be running more smoothly and productively than before. To ensure that changes are integrated throughout the organization, encourage your client to think about the impact of this change on other parts of the client's system. Make sure they have a plan in place to handle turnover of board members, so that when new members are brought on board they will be oriented to the new governing role, make sure organizational policies and bylaws accurately reflect decisions made about the board role, and inform staff and volunteers so that their expectations of the board are appropriate.

Have the project's goals been accomplished?

In Stage 3, we established goals that the organization wanted to achieve during the project. At this time the task is to review those goals and determine the extent to which you've made progress toward them or accomplished them. There are several ways that an organization can go about this assessment:

- Utilize the implementation team, set up in Stage 4, to review progress. In a progress review meeting you might have five agenda items:

  1. Review original goals of the project
  2. Review progress and accomplishments toward achieving those goals
  3. Identify challenges or problem areas that might need attention
  4. Decide how to address challenges: what, who, when
  5. Schedule another progress review meeting in one to two months to check progress again

- Conduct a formal assessment or evaluation of the impact of changes and success of the project. You might want to get information from several people in the organization.

- Hold an informal discussion among the various people or groups involved in the effort to determine progress and the impact of changes.

Step 2: Make Changes or Adjustments as Needed

Hopefully at the conclusion of Step 1 you are able to say with certainty "We have accomplished our goals and our work is done." Congratulations. You are in an enviable situation if that happens. More likely, what you'll realize at the end of Step 1 is that some changes or refinements are needed before you can say that you have successfully completed your work. If this is the case, you might need to go through another cycle of planning and implementation of further changes. Often the changes needed at this stage are minor refinements. However, in some cases they can lead the client into another major planning or change effort, and another consulting project. The steps you would follow would be the same ones outlined in Stages 2, 3, and 4 of the consulting process; that is, you assess exactly what additional work is needed, you develop plans for how you will accomplish that work, and you implement those plans.

The client will often have ongoing refinements or changes to be made to ensure that the project they undertook with you continues to be successful in the future. This leads us into Step 3, which is to help the client set up an ongoing mechanism to monitor their overall progress.

Step 3: Set Up an Ongoing Monitoring Process

Encourage your client to have a mechanism in place for constantly checking their progress toward goals and overall health and wellness, and for creating ways to improve. Establishing this kind of radar system or preventive mechanism will help the client avert crises and problems in the future. It will also help alert them to new opportunities that may arise either internally or externally.

Some organizations, as part of their annual planning process, will have an annual discussion about progress toward goals and challenges or critical issues facing the organization. This can be done formally, through a survey of board and staff, or informally as an agenda item at meetings. Other groups who want to stay on top of issues and concerns more frequently might set aside a little time at the end of every staff or board meeting to "check in" with any concerns that people have.

Peter Senge describes learning organizations as those "where people continually expand their capacity to create the results they truly desire, where new and expansive patterns of thinking are nurtured, where collective aspiration is set free, and where people are continually learning how to learn together.[10] *How* the organization monitors its progress can be tailored to the organization or group's style and needs. The important thing is to help them do it and value it as part of their way of operating.

Step 4: Celebrate Progress and Success

Whatever planning or change effort the organization or group has been involved in, they have put in a lot of time and energy above and beyond their regular level of operations. Individuals are often tired, or even burnt out. They get so caught up in doing, taking on more and more, that they forget to stop and celebrate, play and connect as human beings. Some organizations have traditions of gatherings to celebrate achievements; most rarely think about it. A parting gift you can give your client is a suggestion that they plan a celebration to acknowledge the hard work and contributions of the many people who have been involved in the effort and to celebrate all that has been accomplished through the project. The celebration can be as simple as an impromptu cappuccino and bagels break,

---

[10] Senge, Peter M., *The Fifth Discipline: The Art and Practice of the Learning Organization* (New York: Doubleday, 1990, page 3).

or it can be a picnic in a park for employees and families. It can also be a symbolic gift given to each person who worked hard on the effort. The nature of the celebration is not as important as the gesture of appreciation and the opportunity for the members of the group to plan something that would be of value and fun for them.

Challenges in Stage 5

1. Doing it

It's easy to watch the client get on a roll with their changes or new projects and move on yourself to the next consulting project. If you remember the second goal of consulting—to strengthen the client's capacity to handle similar concerns in the future—you'll have a stronger motivation to, at a minimum, structure a discussion with the client about progress, learnings, and next steps.

2. Instilling a learning orientation

The end of the project isn't a time to sit back and plateau. It is an opportunity to explore how further improvements can be made or new opportunities seized. Help the client make a commitment to continual exploration and improvement. Seeing problems as opportunities, being willing to experiment and fail, having the ability to laugh at oneself, and building the capacity to dream and envision the future are all indicators of a "learning orientation." Watch for these in your client, model them in your own behavior, and support and reinforce any sign of them that you see.

Stage 5 Summary

During Stage 5 you assessed progress, acknowledged accomplishments, and made sure the client had their changes or improvements effectively integrated into the routine operations of the organization or group. You also joined the client in celebrating their achievements. Your work is almost done. It's time now to make an elegant exit.

STAGE 6: Terminating the Consulting Project

Termination involves two components: the formal, deliberate ending of the consulting project and an assessment of your effectiveness as a consultant. You have finished the work that has been agreed upon and all terms of the consulting contract have been met.

Much of the time, termination is simple and straightforward—the work is completed, everyone is satisfied, and consultant and client part ways, at least for this project. Often the relationship continues in a different way—with another consulting project, or because of mutual interest in maintaining a collegial relationship.

Sometimes getting closure is more difficult. At times the consultant resists ending the relationship—the consultant may like the client, enjoy being needed, or believe there is more work to be done. The client may find support or security in leaning on the consultant. I have had former clients who will call me every month or so for lunch—"just to update you on our situation." What they often end up wanting is two or three hours of advice or release. In these cases I've found that a frank talk with the former client is important to clarify whether, and on what terms, to pursue a continuing relationship.

In some cases, there is formal agreement to end the consulting relationship without completing the work. This might occur during any stage of the consulting process. This can occur for a variety of reasons:

The scope of work may be beyond your capabilities

I had a contract to assist an organization in developing a strategic plan with the understanding that the financial projections would be a small part of the plan and would be handled by the finance committee. When we got further into the planning we realized that the main planning issue was finance, and the client needed sophisticated financial modeling and strategy assistance—help that was beyond my capabilities. They only wanted to work with one consultant. I referred them to a financial planning consultant and terminated our relationship.

Emerging events may require termination

In another situation, my consulting contract was to facilitate a creative process with the staff to develop a new program venture. Halfway into the planning, the executive director decided to resign, causing turmoil among the staff and board. We terminated the program planning. When a new director was hired, she charted a different direction for the organization and the program planning was never resumed.

I was assisting a large educational institution with their strategic planning right after they selected a new president—a well-respected scholar with very promising leadership capabilities. After engaging the institution's board, faculty, administration, students, alumni, and other constituents in the early stages of planning, it became clear that the organization was primed for more prominent leadership from its leader. I thought, "I need to fire myself as facilitator of this planning project, and encourage the new president to take a very prominent leadership role for the remainder of the planning. A better role for me might be as coach, if he needs that." He followed this suggestion, proposed an exciting direction for the institution (grounded in what he had heard from others), then worked with appropriate groups to implement this plan. He needed almost no help from me. The institution has thrived. From this project I learned a good bit about two consulting principles: 1) sometimes less help is more helpful, and 2) don't hesitate to change a consulting agreement when the situation requires.

— *Bryan Barry*
Amherst H. Wilder Foundation

You discover a conflict of interest

Many years ago I assisted an organization with planning. As we proceeded through the planning I became more and more uncomfortable with choices they were making, and the values that underpinned those choices. I talked my concerns over with the client and we concluded that I had understood their positions accurately. I was still uncomfortable with their choices and felt hesitant to continue work with them. I ended up terminating the consulting project. The client was respectful of my decision.

There are three straightforward steps to Stage 6. First, you must agree that the consulting relationship has ended. Second, you need to assess the quality of your work. Third, you must finalize client billings and record keeping.

Step 1: Reach Mutual Agreement That the Consulting Relationship Has Ended

Many consulting projects fade gradually away without conscious acknowledgment of the work accomplished and the partnership formed. In addition, most consulting work comes through word-of-mouth referral, so you have an added incentive to end the project with style. Schedule a final meeting with the client to get closure—to make sure that all of their expectations have been met and the work has been done to their satisfaction. In addition, you may want to ask them if they would more formally assess your effectiveness (Step 2) and provide you with a reference for future clients.

At times the decision to terminate the consulting relationship isn't mutual. The client may want more help, support, or coaching and you feel it would not be productive to continue. Or you think the client needs more assistance but they're ready to end the relationship, either because they feel capable of proceeding on their own, or because they don't want the additional expense. In these cases your best approach is to talk frankly with the client and at a minimum make sure you each understand the other's concerns. Different needs for termination often yield rich learnings for both the consultant and client. You may learn something about how the client perceives your strengths and weaknesses and what they have most valued about your work; the client may learn how you assess their capabilities to move forward.

Step 2: Assess Your Effectiveness in the Consultation

When I worked as an independent consultant, I didn't conduct a formal assessment or obtain feedback on my effectiveness. Working in a consulting group that routinely has an outside evaluator interview all completed consulting clients, I've learned to value client feedback about the success of the project and my effectiveness. To help you with your ongoing development as a consultant, Stage 6 is the time to have a discussion with the client about how effectively you have helped them, what you did that was most helpful, and what was least helpful. This can be done through informal discussion with one or more members of the client organization, or more formally through a written evaluation form. Without the luxury of an independent evaluator to conduct an interview, you may question whether you will get honest feedback. In some cases the feedback might not be totally frank, but in most cases, especially where there has been a productive working relationship between you and the client, you will receive valuable information.

Some of the questions you might want to address at this stage are:

- Does the client feel they have been successful in accomplishing their goals?

- If not, what contributed to their lack of success?

- Does the client feel that their ability to handle similar concerns in the future was enhanced?

- What aspect of your work was most useful or helpful?

- What aspect of your work was least helpful?

- Was there anything that you could have done differently that would have been more helpful?

- Was the client satisfied with (make your own list: timeliness, quality, cost, communications, contracting process, billings, facilitation of meetings, materials and reports, etc.)?

- If there was more than one consultant, how effective was each one in providing assistance?

- The next time the client uses a consultant, what would they like to do differently?

Consider developing your own evaluation form, which you ask each client to complete at the conclusion of your work. Having a standard form allows you to track patterns over time and to get feedback from more than one person in an organization. Two sample consulting project evaluation forms are in Appendix D, Consultant Worksheets, on page 201. You'll find them as Worksheets 6 and 7.

Be sensitive to clients who may feel uncomfortable giving you feedback, whether in writing or in person. If the client hesitates you have several choices: you can ask what is behind their hesitation, encourage them by emphasizing that the feedback is for your own professional development, or gracefully let them off the hook.

Step 3: Finalize Client Billings and Record Keeping

If you haven't already, give your client all documents on diskette and hard copy. Make sure that your financial agreements with the client have been met. Send invoices for all work you've done. If there are any disputes about billings, make sure to resolve those as soon as possible. Update any record keeping you maintain on your clients such as mailing lists, phone files, and sample document files. Send your client a thank-you letter and consider asking them if, at some time in the future, they would be comfortable if you used them as a reference.

Chapter Two Summary

The consulting process—the six stages we've worked through in this chapter—is the underlying structure of any consulting project you work on. Keeping these stages in mind and using them as a guide will help you focus on where you are and what the next steps are in your project. This six-stage model of the consulting process has several additional dimensions that you will discover as you gain experience with a variety of projects:

- The consulting process is not always linear. It can be very fluid or elastic, moving back and forth between stages depending on the client's needs and emerging circumstances. The six stages are a way to provide some structure to what is really a more organic discovery process for both the client and consultant.

At times you may need to go back to a previous stage to complete unfinished work, or to take into account new information or events. At times while working on one consulting project you will move into another project, which takes you back to a different stage. Some projects will skip a step or two.

- This consulting process outline can also be used as a problem-solving tool. If you get stuck and aren't sure what to do, go back through the stages of the consulting process, figure out where you are and whether each of the previous stages has been successfully accomplished. If you do find yourself stuck, or if you don't seem to be making progress, it's usually because of unfinished work in a previous stage.

- The stages of the consulting relationship are a lot to absorb if you are new to consulting. Experienced consultants will recognize these stages and will recall the different form and texture they take in each consulting project. Use the stages and steps as a guide but don't follow them as a recipe. Each situation requires an approach tailored to the client's needs.

I've provided two summaries of the stages on pages 105–107 to help you put the pieces together and see how the stages apply in different situations. First is a brief summary of the stages and the steps within each stage (page 105). Second is Figure 10, which shows a summary of how the stages of the consulting process are applied in three different consulting projects. Use this as a final review of the material, and to begin to apply the stages of the consulting project to the type of consulting that you do.

In the next chapter we will discuss aspects of consultation that make it the exciting, creative work that it is. We'll cover consulting roles, the dynamics of change, team consulting, internal and external consulting, and consulting ethics.

Stages of the Consulting Process

STAGE 1: Contracting

Step 1: Understand the Organization and the Work to Be Done

Step 2: Describe Your Background and Experience as a Consultant

Step 3: Begin Developing the Consulting Relationship

Step 4: Develop a Proposal or Written Agreement

Step 5: Decide Whether to Proceed with a Consulting Relationship

STAGE 2: Gathering and Analyzing Data

Step 1: Decide What Information Is Needed and How to Get It

Step 2: Communicate with Various Constituencies about the Data Collection

Step 3: Gather Needed Information

Step 4: Summarize and Analyze Information

Step 5: Share Information with the Organization or Group

STAGE 3: Planning the Work

Step 1: Structure the Planning Process

Step 2: Identify Key Issues

Step 3: Define Goals

Step 4: Develop Strategies

Step 5: Prepare an Implementation Plan

STAGE 4: Implementing and Monitoring

Step 1: Complete Implementation Activities

Step 2: Attend to Communication and Participation

Step 3: Monitor and Make Adjustments throughout the System

STAGE 5: Sustaining Change and Evaluating Impact

Step 1: Review Progress or Results in Achieving Goals

Step 2: Make Changes or Adjustments as Needed

Step 3: Set Up an Ongoing Monitoring Process

Step 4: Celebrate Progress and Success

STAGE 6: Terminating the Consulting Project

Step 1: Reach Mutual Agreement That the Consulting Relationship Has Ended

Step 2: Assess Your Effectiveness in the Consultation

Step 3: Finalize Client Billings and Record Keeping

Figure 10	Application of the Stages of the Consulting Process in Three Different Consulting Projects		

Stages of the Consulting Process:

The Consulting Project	STAGE 1: Contracting	STAGE 2: Gathering and Analyzing Data	STAGE 3: Planning the Work
Board Planning Retreat *You are asked to design and facilitate an annual nonprofit board planning retreat.*	You meet with the executive director and board chair to discuss their goals for the retreat and the scope of plans they wish to develop. You recommend doing a brief survey of board and staff prior to the retreat to collect ideas. They also want you to summarize the retreat discussion into a first draft plan. You send them a letter confirming the retreat goals, tentative agenda, description of your role, and the cost. They call to confirm.	You review past organizational plans and relevant documents. You survey board and staff to gain their ideas about current challenges and future opportunities, and summarize the responses. You generate a list of possible critical issues and opportunities to be addressed in planning.	You revise the retreat agenda based on information gathered, getting approval from the executive committee. The organization sends out meeting packets. You plan event details such as space, equipment, meals, presentations, handouts, exercises.
Merger *You are asked to help two nonprofit organizations move through a possible merger process.*	The executive director of one agency calls you. After determining that you have the skills and interest, they invite you for an interview with the board chairs and executive directors of the two agencies. They are also interviewing other consultants. You submit a brief outline of a possible merger process. They select you to work with them. You submit a lengthy proposal, work plan, and budget, which they accept.	A merger committee made up of representatives of both organizations is formed. The merger committee members orient you and determine information that is needed to inform their boards' decisions. You and the committee members collect information.	You hold a series of joint board meetings to explore goals, opportunities, and risks. The boards decide to proceed with the merger. (If the boards had decided not to proceed you would have moved to Stage 6: Terminating the Consulting Project.) The merger committee develops a merger implementation plan, with staff input, which is approved by both boards.
Neighborhood Focus Groups *You are asked to design and conduct focus groups with neighborhood residents to get their input on a proposed playground.*	A neighborhood association has heard about you and wants you to conduct and report on eight focus groups to get community input on proposed plans for a playground. They have the questions they want answered. You meet, discuss their goals, ideas, and your availability, and agree to the work. You confirm the agreement in a letter outlining goals, number of focus groups, format of final report, and cost.	Because the nature of the work is assessment, there is little prior assessment needed before the planning begins. However, you do find it necessary to clarify information needs from potential funders or decision makers and to refine focus group questions.	You meet with the neighborhood association once to clarify the information needed, the audience, scope, and format for the report; the invitation list; and the process and logistics for the focus groups. You develop a detailed focus group agenda.

STAGE 4: Implementing and Monitoring	STAGE 5: Sustaining Change and Evaluating Impact	STAGE 6: Terminating the Consulting Project
You conduct the retreat as planned. Halfway through the retreat a hot issue emerges that needs to be resolved. You ask the group whether they want to spend retreat time working on the issue or resolve it later. They want to resolve it now so you renegotiate the retreat agenda (back to Stage 3), and then continue with the revised agenda. After the retreat you draft plans that were developed in the retreat.	You meet with the board chair and executive director to review the summary plan and discuss how the retreat went. At their request you make recommendations for steps they might take to complete the planning. (If they want help with some of these steps, you are prepared to begin again back at Stage 1.)	You agree that the work as defined in your consulting agreement or contract is concluded. You ask the client for feedback on your work, and suggestions for how you could have improved your service. You send a final bill if you are charging them for the work.
You serve as advisor and facilitator to the two organizations as they move through the merger process. This work takes nearly two years. At bimonthly meetings the merger committee assesses progress and adjusts implementation steps as needed.	One year after the merger is formalized you and the merger committee review progress against goals and determine further adjustments that are needed.	You agree that the work as defined in your consulting agreement or contract is concluded. You ask the client for feedback (as you've done regularly on a project this long) on your work. You send a final bill if you are charging them for the work.
The neighborhood association sends out invitations and makes site arrangements. You conduct the focus groups as planned. After the first two focus groups you adjust the agenda and questions because you ran short of time in the first two. You summarize the information gathered into the agreed upon report format.	You review the report with the neighborhood association, clarifying any items that are not clear. You help them determine the usefulness of the focus groups and whether additional information is needed.	You agree that the work as defined in your consulting agreement or contract is concluded. You ask the client for feedback on your work. You send a final bill if you are charging them for the work.

CHAPTER THREE

Artistry

Consulting Roles, Dynamics, and Ethics

We will now explore some aspects of the consulting role that add artistry
to what you do. We'll look at the wide variety of roles that a consultant can
play, whether in different consulting projects or from one meeting to the
next in the same consulting project. We'll explore the dynamics of change
in organizations and the consultant's role in facilitating change. We'll
discuss working with co-consultants—the advantages and disadvantages
of consulting teams. The differences between internal and external consulting will be explored for those of you who serve as consultants within
your organizations. And finally we'll study some ethical dilemmas that
consultants often face, and how to think these through.

Consulting Roles

Who is the consultant? One consultant sits in a corner of the room during
a board meeting and never says anything. Another consultant works with
staff of a neighborhood organization nearly full time for two months planning a neighborhood celebration. Another consultant meets one-on-one

with an executive director weekly to coach her. And a fourth consultant mediates a dispute between two staff departments. Which one is the real consultant?

The answer is, of course, probably all of them. A consultant can take on many roles, differing from project to project, from meeting to meeting, or even during one meeting. A consultant might serve as a trainer, facilitator, educator, researcher, coach, expert, role model, sounding board, confronter, or mediator. When is one role used over another? How do you decide what kind of role is needed at any one time, or with a particular consulting project?

Here are five factors that determine the kind of role a consultant chooses:

1. *Skills*

   Some consultants tend to work in one role—for example, as a trainer or a researcher—throughout their career. They have honed their skills in training or research and don't have experience in other roles. They will usually take on only those consulting projects that make use of their strengths.

2. *Style preference*

   Some consultants are more comfortable with certain roles than others, either because that's where they feel their strengths are or because they believe that's the most effective way to influence the client. For example, many consultants are uncomfortable serving in the "expert" role because they believe it creates dependency on the client's part and does not build ownership for the issues or solutions in the project. Other consultants may use the expert role the majority of the time because that is their comfort zone. They are less at ease with a participative creative process. (I'll talk more about these style differences—from *expert* to *reflector*—later in this section.)

3. *Client preference*

   At times clients will specify the kind of role they want a consultant to play. They might ask you to do research and bring in best-practice ideas from projects around the country. They might ask you to serve as a facilitator for only part of a meeting, because they want their board chair to retain overall leadership. Or they may specify that you conduct an assessment of their supervisory practices, feed back that information to the organization, and finally assist the organization in developing change strategies based on the findings. In this case the consultant serves both as a data gatherer and a facilitator of the client's decision about how to respond to the data.

4. *The nature of the project*

The nature of the work to be done may dictate certain roles. For example, a group of organizations wants help forming an alliance to influence policymakers. They have one week to respond to pending legislation, and they are in conflict about what position to take. The consultant doesn't have time for leisurely data collection or planning. The group needs to come together, identify optional positions, weigh them, and form a decision quickly.

5. *The needs of the group or organization*

Because of challenges facing the organization or dynamics present in the group, the consultant might determine that a certain kind of role is needed in order to be most helpful on a project. For example, a board might become stuck in circular thinking—they aren't considering new ideas from outside their group. You decide that being a challenger to the closed thinking process is what would get the group moving again. In another case, a conflict emerges that requires mediation before the group can continue with their planning activities.

These five factors determine the role or roles needed in any consulting project. You can see that the first two factors, skills and style preference, really depend upon the consultant; the third, client preference, depends upon the client; and the fourth and fifth factors, the nature of the project and needs of the group, depend upon the project. As you might imagine, the last two are also the least apparent, most variable factors. Most consulting projects I've worked on are complex enough that I've needed to shift roles during the project—mostly due to the changing nature of the project or the needs of the group. In fact, during a project a consultant might play numerous roles, depending on what's happening at that point in time.

We often end up changing our role in midstream on a project. In one situation, thirty arts groups hired us to come in and do a series of trainings. Most of the topics they wanted were in pretty standard areas. One of them, on media savvy, was new to us. We knew we could do a good job on the others but we would have to bring in some people we didn't know to do the media session. As we talked further, we discovered that they had the resources in the room to do their own training in that area. They only needed us to facilitate a couple of meetings to draw forth the issues they wanted to cover. We recontracted and instead of bringing in people to conduct training, we became the designers. We've learned not just to check in and make sure the client is happy but to see if the job is taking a turn, to revisit the contract and make sure we are going in the right direction. This was also an interesting example of using a combination of internal and external resources to get the job done.

— *Karen Simmons*
Director, LaSalle University Nonprofit Center and President, Nonprofit Management Association

Because of the fluidity of Factors 4 and 5, most consultants sooner or later come to these three realizations:

1. It's important to have comfort and skills in a wide range of roles to be most effective.

2. It's important to have the ability to determine or diagnose when different roles are called for, or when it's appropriate to change roles.

3. It's important to monitor continually the impact of your role, to make sure you are having the intended effect.

If we think only about Factors 4 and 5—the ones that might cause us to change roles in the middle of a project—then it's clear we need some guideposts for figuring out when to change, and what role to change to. Each role has advantages and limitations, depending on what needs to be accomplished. Let's look more closely now at the situations where the different consulting roles might be used, as well as the advantages and disadvantages of each.

The Continuum of Consulting Roles[11]

One way to think about consulting roles is to imagine them spread over a continuum. In Figure 11, the left side of the continuum describes roles that are more directive or that place more emphasis on the consultant's special-ized knowledge and experience. These can be called *consultant-centered* roles. On the right side of the continuum are consultant roles that are nondirective; that is, they place more emphasis on eliciting the client's experience and knowledge. These are *client-centered* roles.

The continuum represents a range of different roles that vary by the relative balance of influence the consultant and client are exercising. On the left, the consultant exercises more influence; on the right, the client exercises more influence. You can also think of the chart as showing a continuum of *situations* where the roles might be called for. If you are asked to do conflict resolution, you might use a variety of roles to facilitate the resolution of the conflict.

There are five categories of roles on the continuum:

- Advocate
- Expert
- Educator or trainer
- Catalyst
- Reflector

---

[11] Gordon Lippit and Ronald Lippit offer a comprehensive exploration of consulting roles and criteria for choosing a particular role in their book *The Consulting Process in Action* (San Francisco: Jossey-Bass, 1986, pp. 57-63).

Each of these roles will be described below, along with their uses and limitations. For illustration's sake, I'll describe the ends of the continuum—advocate and reflector—as extremes. Note that few consultants will actually operate in those extreme ways.

Consultant Roles   **Figure 11**

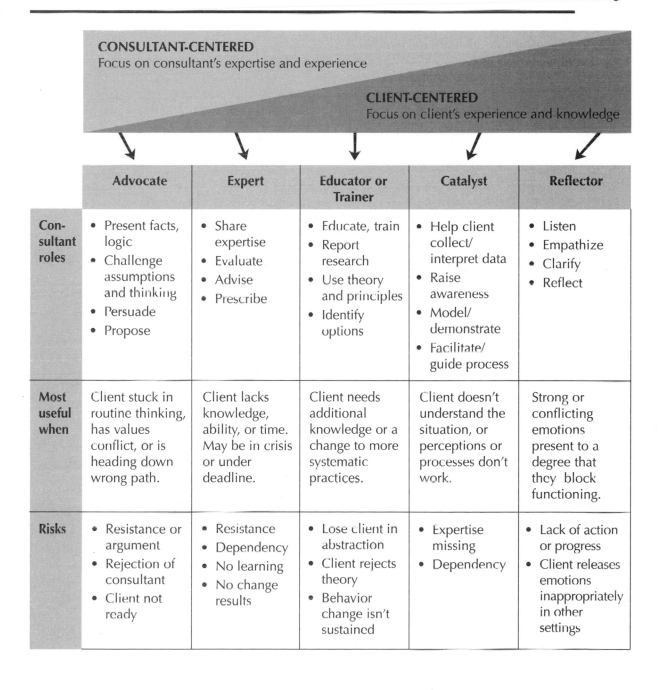

	Advocate	**Expert**	**Educator or Trainer**	**Catalyst**	**Reflector**
Consultant roles	• Present facts, logic • Challenge assumptions and thinking • Persuade • Propose	• Share expertise • Evaluate • Advise • Prescribe	• Educate, train • Report research • Use theory and principles • Identify options	• Help client collect/ interpret data • Raise awareness • Model/ demonstrate • Facilitate/ guide process	• Listen • Empathize • Clarify • Reflect
Most useful when	Client stuck in routine thinking, has values conflict, or is heading down wrong path.	Client lacks knowledge, ability, or time. May be in crisis or under deadline.	Client needs additional knowledge or a change to more systematic practices.	Client doesn't understand the situation, or perceptions or processes don't work.	Strong or conflicting emotions present to a degree that they block functioning.
Risks	• Resistance or argument • Rejection of consultant • Client not ready	• Resistance • Dependency • No learning • No change results	• Lose client in abstraction • Client rejects theory • Behavior change isn't sustained	• Expertise missing • Dependency	• Lack of action or progress • Client releases emotions inappropriately in other settings

CONSULTANT-CENTERED
Focus on consultant's expertise and experience

CLIENT-CENTERED
Focus on client's experience and knowledge

Advocate

On the far left end of the continuum is the advocate role. The consultant acting as an advocate exerts strong influence on the client, urging them to think or act in a certain way. When acting as an advocate, the consultant tries to influence the client to act or think in a certain way. I use the advocate role most often when I see a discrepancy between words and action, when the client seems stuck, or when I have content expertise or strong opinions about how the client might proceed. For instance, the client may say they value something, but exhibit behavior that is inconsistent with those values. Or, the organization claims to value diversity, but they don't have diverse staff or programs that are accessible to the communities they serve. In this instance, you as consultant might choose to take an advocacy role to help the client see the contradiction.

Another form of advocacy might be called for when a consultant sees tension between two people that is blocking a whole organization or group from moving forward. In this case, I think that the greatest value I can give to my client is to say the unsayable or unpopular—to point out the "elephant in the living room." This might involve giving feedback to someone in private when their behavior is disruptive, or challenging a board chair to make a decision. I use a direct advocate role when I've exhausted every other reasonable attempt to move the client ahead.

The big risk of being an advocate is that the client may resist, become defensive, or lose confidence, because they refuse to accept your premise. They may also reject what you say because you chose the wrong moment to confront the issue. If you confront a situation five minutes before a dinner break, for instance, the group won't deal with it. You have to think of timing in a larger sense too—the success of your advocacy is affected by the developmental stage of the organization and the openness to feedback of the people concerned.

When using advocacy, the client may simply not "hear" you at first. You may get resistance the first or second or even third time you say something, but it doesn't mean you should stop confronting what in your best judgment needs confronting. Say it in a different way, use different examples, present the issue to different people, use humor—just work to keep the issue alive in a gentle way with the client.

Ultimately, though, the biggest risk is outright rejection by the client. A client may reject getting the outside assistance they need. They may try to protect the reality they know, because it *is* known and because it's comfortable. The value you add by confronting a situation might not be felt or understood for some time in the organization. Your contract could be terminated, or you might become identified with the problem you have pointed out and turned into the scapegoat for whatever further troubles the group has. It's important here to remember that this response is not personal.

Expert

Expert roles, toward the left on the continuum, are also consultant-centered. They focus on the consultant's expertise, beliefs, and knowledge. In the purest form of this role category, the consultant is the expert—someone who has information or perspective that the client wants. Different ways of being an expert include prescribing a course of action, evaluating, or advising. In the classic expert consulting role, a consultant will come into the client system, study the situation, and recommend a course of action. The client is then free to choose to follow the recommendation or not. If the consultant has effectively studied the situation, and if the client agrees with the consultant's findings and recommendations, respects the consultant's expertise, and has the ability to implement the recommendations, this can be an effective role and action will likely result.

Expert roles are most useful when a client lacks time, ability, or knowledge, or—for whatever reason—is unable to act on their own. Expert roles are also useful when the client is in crisis, at the end of their rope. If they are at a peak of frustration with a situation, they may need to have someone come in and tell them what to do so they can start moving.

There are risks inherent in expert roles. The consultant could come to a faulty conclusion or have inaccurate information—and thus lead the client astray. And because it is so consultant-centered, the expert role is less likely either to build the client's capacity to handle similar situations in the future, or to create acceptance by the organization for either the problem or the plans that are created to solve it. This role also often creates resistance, defensiveness, or dependency. The greatest risk, then, is that no learning occurs and no change results.

Educator or trainer

At the midpoint of the continuum is the third category of consultant roles, the educator or trainer. These roles balance or share power between the consultant and the client. The educator or trainer brings information (in the form of research, theoretical material, principles that have been used elsewhere, or training programs) and works collaboratively with the client to apply them to the client's situation. Typical roles included in this category are trainer, teacher, coach, and researcher.

A consultant could be brought in to train a board in governance. Or a consultant might be hired to research low-income housing models for transitional neighborhoods. In these cases, the consultant will try to understand what the client is interested in learning and then design a data gathering, training, or reporting process that will meet their needs. As consultant acting in this role, you don't necessarily give recommendations, answers, or solutions; you provide information and assist the client in finding their own solutions. As a coach a consultant might assist a client in thinking through what they're doing and identifying choices or courses of action. The consultant offers information to inform and expand the client's thinking.

An educational intervention can be a small part of a larger project in which you are acting in another role. For example, let's say you're facilitating a neighborhood planning meeting and the group is stuck on how to make a decision about priority goals for the neighborhood. In that situation, you might take thirty minutes for a short educational piece on decision making. You introduce five ways for a group to make decisions and help the group decide how they're going to decide on their goals. Then you can move back into the facilitator role for the actual decision making. The client has half the power—you give them options, they choose what they're going to do and how they're going to do it.

Trainer and educator roles are typically used when a client group wants to enhance their current functioning through new information. I've utilized this role when the client expressed interest either in being more systematic (less chaotic, more informed) about their practices or in expanding the range of knowledge and understanding about their organization or program. For example, during a strategic planning project, the client wants to know how other groups across the country are addressing the same or similar issues. Or, a community development corporation hires a consultant to find out how other community development corporations set up loan funds to help with renovation.

Trainer and educator roles are most effective when there is follow-up involvement between the client and the consultant to ensure that the theory and principles are applied and that change happens as a result of the learning that has taken place.

The risks inherent in this role include the possibility of losing the client in abstraction, when the client isn't able to apply the outside information to their own situation. Second, the client may reject a theory because they don't think it's valid. Third, the client may agree with an approach suggested by an outside source in principle but isn't able to follow through applying it to their organization.

Catalyst

Closer to the right end of the continuum is the catalytic consultant role. In this category, the consultant is a catalyst to help the client take action. The assumption is that the client has experience and knowledge to do what they need to do, but for some reason needs a spark lit under them to actually do it. Or they need something to help them keep moving, or to guide the process so that they can all participate. In the catalytic role, a consultant might collect new information, demonstrate a different behavior or a new way of doing things, or provide feedback on group dynamics—all to give the client the spark for change.

Catalytic roles are most appropriate when a client has difficulty accomplishing something, when they don't understand all the factors contributing to a situation, or don't know where or how to get information. Sometimes they've been doing things a certain way for a long time but they don't realize they're in a rut. Sometimes the client might simply need to have a little creative jolt. Here the consultant is using minimal power and expertise to help the client do what they want to do.

An example of a common catalytic role is facilitation. Facilitation means to make something easier, or at least less difficult. The role of facilitator is to create and sustain an environment in which the group can accomplish its task and learn about itself in the process.[12] A facilitator will commonly lead a group through some process to achieve their goals, usually without asserting undue influence or guidance on the content of the group's work.

Catalytic roles are related to advocacy roles, but differ in style. In advocacy, the consultant comes off much more as an expert or authority ("You need to do this" or "You should...") and in some cases even poses possible consequences ("If you don't change, this will happen"). In a catalytic role, on the other hand, the consultant makes an observation about something that's happening ("I have noticed...") and then suggests changes that the client might want to consider making ("Let me suggest some options"). Note the style difference, though the goal—to move the client out of a difficult place toward change—is similar. The final decision is always up to the client—you support them in the path they choose but help them understand the consequences of the decision. As a catalyst you are continuously trying to build the client's own expertise and knowledge. You give them what you can of yours, rather than trying to hold onto it.

A big risk of the catalytic consulting roles is that it's easy to stay at the surface level of an issue, not analyzing deeply what the challenges are. In catalytic consulting, you're putting the majority of the weight on the client's skills and knowledge. Even when everyone in the client group

---

[12] Keltner, J.R. (1989) "Facilitation: Catalyst for Group Problem Solving." *Communication Quarterly* 3 (1) 8-32.

agrees on a strategy, you may well end up asking: is it really the best strategy—do they have the expertise to address the really hard questions?

In addition, in the catalytic roles, the consultant is so supportive of the client's strengths and skills that it's easy to cause dependency. That is, the client wants the consultant to be around constantly to provide the creative nudge or that insightful piece of feedback to move them along. You, as the consultant, have to make sure the client is gradually learning how to do the work on their own.

Reflector

At the far right end of the continuum is the reflector role. In a reflector role, the consultant will rely almost totally on a client's experience and knowledge, and little on his or her own. The role of the consultant here is to be a sounding board and a mirror. As the consultant, you are there to listen, reflect what you hear, empathize, and support the client. You describe what you hear or observe so the client can clarify their own thinking, decisions, or solutions.

I often use reflection with individuals or with informal groups, rather than in consultation to an entire organization or collaborative. Using the reflector role, I might work one-on-one with an executive director who is having difficulty resolving a recurrent conflict in the organization. Or perhaps my client is a neighborhood group that is upset about a city council decision. The group simply wants a chance to vent their feelings to someone and get help organizing their thinking before they respond to the city council. Using reflection, I don't suggest options; I only listen and tell the client what I'm hearing.

I also find that the reflector role is useful when strong emotions are present—typically, when logic and facts just won't work. Organizations and groups experience loss of staff from downsizing, illness, or death; anger about forces affecting them from within or outside the organization; or stress due to workload or economic downturns. Sometimes you might notice that such "history" seems to be preventing a focus on the future—prompting you to say something like "It seems that what's happened over the years is still alive in the group." Even if the group goes on, your job is to stop them every so often and just "name" the behavior. By putting a label on what's happening, you encourage the release of thoughts or feelings that are getting in the way of effective functioning. You simply listen, encourage talking, and feed back what you hear so that the group can hear and work it through.

As you can see, the reflector role borders on what a psychologist or therapist might do, and therein lies the biggest risk. Most consultants are not therapists and don't have the training to deal with psychological issues. Using this type of role without having the skills to know when an individual's or group's emotions are deeply rooted or potentially destructive can be risky. In this role, a consultant needs to be able to recognize the line between healthy emoting (which may serve to move the group forward and improve their functioning) and acting as a therapist or counselor, helping people through their personal problems. Clearly, you can quickly cross the line from an appropriate organizational focus to an inappropriate personal focus without the skills to handle what might come out.

I once had an experience that taught me the importance of being clear about my role as a consultant and maintaining clear boundaries between personal and professional roles. I was working with an organization where there was significant conflict between the executive director and associate director. I focused on strengthening team effectiveness and work group processes. The sessions were intense and a lot of emotional issues were being worked through. I was very surprised when, independently, both the director and associate director approached me for a date. This made me suspect that the personal nature of the work we were doing had been misinterpreted as personal interest. I learned several things from this situation. First, I need to pay close attention to boundary management, especially in emotion-laden situations. In looking for opportunities to get insight into the conflict, I had gone down personal paths. I'm less willing now to have conversations that are counselor-like. I'm clear with clients that that is not the work that I do. I keep a clear focus on work issues, and keep talking to the client about whether the work we set out to do is getting done. Second, I keep a clearer focus on who is responsible for making change. I had in effect joined them in their struggle and was invested in seeing change happen. With more experience it's easier for me to sense when relationships are getting out of whack.

— *Mike Allison, Director of Consulting Services*
Support Center for Nonprofit Management

Another risk is in so successfully offering your client safety and support that they go on to "release" or emote inappropriately in other settings, expecting the same support and safety. That is, they might emote all over the mayor's desk or expect unconditional understanding from their board chair.

The continuum of consulting roles is a tool to help you understand the repertoire of roles available to you, develop greater role flexibility, choose roles that may be needed at different times in consulting projects, and observe the impact your role might be having on the client or the consulting project progress.

Remember the three rules of roles that will help you enhance your effectiveness as a consultant:

1. It's important to feel at ease with and have skills in a wide range of roles.

2. It's important to have the ability to determine when it's appropriate to change roles.

3. It's important to monitor continually the impact of your role to make sure you are having the intended effect.

It can take a while to find a role and style that will work with a client. We were working with a grassroots coalition of community-building groups focused on family and children's issues. We sent over one consultant who did a good job but the chemistry wasn't that good with the client. The project started to fall apart. When we sent the third month's bill they didn't pay it. We sent in a different consultant to bring some of the strings together. This consultant didn't mesh either. Finally the group called back a couple months later, and we sent in a third consultant, one who had a much better sense of working with grassroots groups. This consulting project went well. It's a totally different contract from the first. The goals and dollars were the same, but the style, checkpoints and tasks were different. We learned a couple of things from this project. If we hadn't been careful about recontracting we may have been tempted to use the original contract, instead of looking at a different way to approach the project. The second thing we learned had to do with style. Originally they thought they wanted an expert to come in and give advice. We told them that's not our philosophy, that we wanted to help them develop their own capacity. They said that they were okay with that. But then we saw them doing things badly. The expert role was needed, and the consultant had to turn into an expert advisor after all. Our typical consulting approach wouldn't work because they didn't have the time it would take. We had said we would do it one way and then we did it the other way—and by then they really didn't want the advice, didn't agree with it, and didn't own it. The consultant who is working with them now understands that and can blend styles. We offer advice and options and the client can choose not to use it. There's a mutual respect built in from the start.

— *Karen Simmons*
Director, LaSalle University Nonprofit Center and President, Nonprofit Management Association

Summary of Consultant Roles

Advocate   The **advocate** role challenges a client to examine how their present thinking or assumptions may be affecting the way situations are viewed. The consultant attempts to influence the client to consider a different approach or pinpoints assumptions that are blocking their functioning. The consultant may probe, challenge, give feedback, or offer logic in such a way that the client doesn't feel attacked or put down. The consultant brings her or his expertise or knowledge to bear on the client's situation.

Expert

In the **expert** role, the consultant tells a client what to do or does it for them. The consultant develops evidence or rationale for the problem, advises the client about the best course of action, and sometimes implements the solution. The consultant's aim is to give the client needed guidance or conviction. This role is most useful when the client is in a crisis, urgently needs to make decisions, or doesn't have the information needed to take action.

Educator or trainer

By offering information, research, or alternatives pertinent to the client's situation, or training the client in specific skills, the consultant in the role of a **trainer or educator** helps the client strengthen their understanding of a situation or their skills in handling it. The client then becomes able to deal with present and future situations more effectively. The consultant and client work in partnership to address the issues.

Catalyst

A consultant working as a **catalyst** assists the client in moving along their process or gaining a broader understanding of their concerns. Primary consultant skills include facilitation, process consultation, action research, modeling, survey feedback, and coaching. The catalyst role more actively intervenes in the client's world than the reflector role, but still relies on the client's knowledge and expertise.

Reflector

A consultant working as a **reflector** assists the client in moving through feelings or conflicts that may be causing them difficulty. The consultant provides a safe environment and process that respects the client and helps them work through their concerns. Active listening, assistance in clarifying issues and exploring alternatives, and empathetic support are the main consultant behaviors.

The Dynamics of Change in the Consulting Process

Consulting is a relationship with an organization or group seeking to bring about change. As with any change process, consulting is always unpredictable and ultimately a creative process. Working on a goal to create new understandings, capabilities, systems, ways of doing things, or relationships can be exciting or stressful for people in the client system and can require great creativity and sensitivity on the part of the consult-ant. A consultant needs an understanding of how people react to change and how a consultant can help make the change process productive.

William Bridges conceptualizes transition as a three-phase psychological reorientation process that most individuals or groups experience.[13] The first stage is endings, or death of the old ways of doing or being. The second stage is the neutral zone, a time between the past and the future, when there is uncertainty and a readjustment to the possibility of something new. The third stage is beginnings or birth of the new, the time for starting new things. See Figure 12 below.

Figure 12   **How People Experience Transition**

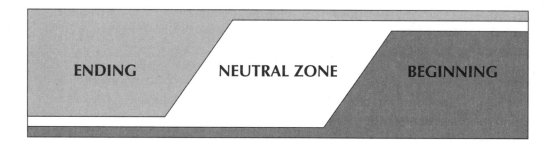

People move through these three stages in different ways and at different paces. Some people are ready to let go of the past and embrace the new quickly; others need time, information, and reassurance about the change before they are ready to get on board. For some people, or with certain kinds of change, it is an emotional process and they need a lot of support and encouragement; for other people or with changes that are easier to understand, change is logical and attractive and doesn't arouse emotions.

Ideally, in your consulting role, you can help facilitate a process that will create an openness to change within the organization, ownership of the change goals and plans among all stakeholders, and a learning orientation so that people are open to ongoing discovery and improvement. This kind of environment will help individuals move through their individual pro-cess of transition. There are several ways as a consultant that you can foster and encourage this kind of environment and ownership of the change process. There are also several dynamics that sometimes occur during change which you need to be sensitive to.

---

[13] Reprinted with special permission of William Bridges, author of *Managing Transitions: Making the Most of Change* (Reading, Mass.: Addison-Wesley Publishing Company, 1991, page 70).

Ownership

A consultant has a choice of roles; each role has strengths and limitations. Organizations or groups that have strong leadership or expertise will need less direction, will benefit from a more client-centered approach, and will likely have greater ownership of the change plans and outcomes. A more directive or consultant-centered approach may be appropriate with groups who tend to get stuck easily, have weak leadership, or are in a time crunch, but it generally does not result in the client organization feeling a sense of ownership of the data or decisions; the data and decisions may be viewed as belonging to the consultant. Many organizations or groups will want the consultant to tell them what is "good" and "bad," and what they should do. They will want recommendations, and there are times when it is appropriate and necessary for the consultant to make recommendations, to tell the client what you think they should do. There is a risk, though, that the client can become dependent on you to guide the effort and provide leadership, instead of building the leadership within the client system.

To build ownership of the change effort, it needs to be *their* discovery process. You, as a consultant, can contribute expertise or provide needed skills or time, but the process belongs to the client. Following are some ways that you can help build and sustain client ownership of and commitment to change:

1. Don't do anything for a client that they can do for themselves. A related guideline is to make sure that you are not working harder than the client. Look for opportunities for the client to take the lead, or at least work with you.

2. Make sure the client is getting the full benefit of your wisdom and experience, but not in a way that minimizes their own experience. Ask them for their ideas before offering your own. If you do make recommendations, let the group work with the issues first, and provide your recommendations only after they have developed some ideas.

3. Make sure that the group or organization is making their own decisions. Your job is to help them understand the pros and cons of different choices and to help them implement the decisions they make.

4. Build anticipation and excitement within the group about the discovery or learning process. Position the information and process that you contribute as a gift that poses opportunities and choices for them to decide their future.

Openness to Change and Learning

Part of the goal of consultation is that the organization or group learns skills or processes to deal more effectively with future challenges as they emerge, ways to maintain a healthy state of adaptability to changing conditions, and how to maximize the strengths and resources in the group for ongoing creative improvements. Part of transition, according to Bridges, involves letting go of the old ways or ideas. Different people work through transition in different ways. Some of the dynamics that can be experienced during change are described in the following section.

People can sometimes get overwhelmed by or anxious about change. They might be uncomfortable with change, not understand why change is occurring, or feel that their ideas or experience are not being heard. This is commonly referred to as resistance to change. Resistance is often a clue to some important piece of information that needs to be heard, understood, and attended to in order to make the change effort succeed. Other writers have explored the dynamic of resistance in depth. A good source is Peter Block's book, *Flawless Consulting*.[14] Defensiveness occurs when an individual or group feels that they are being judged or threatened in some way. Defensive behavior is a way of protecting themselves from a real or perceived threat. When people are protecting themselves they are generally not open to learning and are not contributing their best to the group's efforts. Protection becomes more important than learning. Defensiveness and resistance are normal, valuable, and sometimes difficult dynamics in any change process and should not be dismissed or ignored.

Resistance and defensiveness manifest themselves in many ways, including: focus on details, reality tests ("that isn't going to work"), attacks and arguing, anger, confusion, silence, intellectualizing, moralizing, passive compliance, feeling judged, obsession with process or methodology, escape into health (high illness rates), or insistence on solutions. The challenge in responding to these behaviors is to see them as valuable parts of the process, rather than interference coming from people who have something "wrong" with them. People who respond in this way are doing what seems appropriate given their needs and their view of reality. To make the change process succeed, respond to resistance or defensiveness immediately, directly, and authentically using the following guidelines.

1. Notice resistance or defensiveness, listen for what a person or group needs beyond what they might be saying, and describe what you are observing.

2. Ask people to identify what they would like to happen or to describe one change that would be most important for them.

---

[14] Block, Peter, *Flawless Consulting* (Austin, Tex.: Learning Concepts, 1981).

3. Adjust the process or approach to incorporate their concerns, if possible.

4. If, after repeated attempts to work constructively with people's concerns, the project is not progressing, assist the group or organization in deciding how to proceed. Include consideration of options to stop the project, proceed in a different way, or proceed without the involvement of people who don't support the effort.

Your challenge is to use your role and relationship with the client to help transform dependency, defensiveness, and resistance, when they occur, into corresponding strengths of ownership, learning orientation, and openness to change.

Dependency ➡ Ownership

Defensiveness ➡ Learning orientation

Resistance ➡ Openness to change

Team Consulting

Many consultants are lone rangers. They get into consulting, among other reasons, because they really like to work alone and be their own boss. As we discussed in Chapter 1, a good share of the consulting done in the nonprofit sector is done by independent consultants. Another large portion is done by nonprofit management support organizations and consulting groups. Whether consultants are working on their own or working with a group of other consultants, much of the consulting work they do will be solo work. Whether to work on a particular project solo or as a team is a relevant question for independent consultants and those part of an MSO or consulting group.

In the nonprofit sector the main reason for the predominance of solo consulting is cost. Working with more than one consultant on a project increases the cost for the client (unless the consultants are doing different things, or both consultants are willing to cut their rates in half). Nevertheless, there are times when team consulting makes a lot of sense and in fact is necessary to navigate the challenges of a project.

Working with a partner is appropriate in some situations and inappropriate in others.[15] Let's look first at the situations where team consulting might be important.

---

[15] Jeanette Milgrom and Gary Schoener of Walk-In Counseling, Minneapolis, Minnesota, helped develop these ideas on team consultation during the early 1980s.

You Might Want to Work with One or More Partner Consultants When . . .

1. Personal characteristics or backgrounds are complementary

If there are different personal characteristics that are important—either to the client or because of the nature of the work—these characteristics ought to be reflected in the consulting team. For example, you might want to team a male consultant with a female consultant, a younger person with an older person, gay with straight, African American with Caucasian, or professional with paraprofessional.

> Sometimes working as a team on a project is necessary for the success of the work. I once worked with a small hospital and clinic in a rural area helping them look at how they could position themselves in an area served by larger hospitals. They needed complex analysis of a lot of data, skills I don't have. They ended up bringing in a marketing consultant to collect data as part of the planning, while I handled the planning process. We had to deal with lots of quantitative information, and that information ended up being crucial to the effectiveness of the planning. Information from the broader market gave us a much better and broader base to make decisions. I learned how important it is to be honest about my lack of personal expertise in marketing research. The marketing consultant and I probably could've been more clear about what our respective roles were, but having two of us was important for the success of the project.
>
> — *Terry Donovan*
> *Independent Consultant*

Similarly, you might need a team approach when consultants represent different viewpoints or disciplines. The consultants might individually represent backgrounds in administration, finance, or program expertise. Or, for example, in working with a mental health agency, different consultants might bring the viewpoints of family therapy, individual therapy, or group therapy. In these cases, the purpose of having contrasting viewpoints might be to invite open debate or to model ways of getting along.

Finally, consultants might have complementary styles of working. One consultant may tend to lecture, the other may have skills in experiential learning. Or one is serious and businesslike and the other is warm and uses humor to create openness in a group.

> Sometimes two consultants are necessary for success of a project. We were working with an AIDS group, which can be incredibly difficult. Everything is life and death, and it happens quickly. Relationships are contentious; tempers flare easily. It's difficult work but fulfilling in the end. The AIDS group wanted a strategic plan. There were a lot of political and emotional undertones. The board president was distrustful of the executive director, and throughout the planning process we suspected the board president was trying to dig up information that could get the director fired. So the contract was to develop a strategic plan, but as soon as we got in there we saw so much infighting that had to be dealt with. Having two consultants on the project was impor-
>
> tant: one to push along the planning process, and one to deal with the political infighting and the lack of trust. One person alone wouldn't have been able to get through it, wouldn't have had the energy to sustain it. One of us represented the executive director in mediation sessions; the other represented the board chair. The group refused to stop fighting, yet they wanted to keep on task. Usually when the group is conflicted we will put the planning process on hold temporarily and resolve issues that are getting in the way. We ended up getting through the planning, and they loved the plan. But it took two of us to help them get through it.
>
> — *Karen Simmons*
> *Director, LaSalle University Nonprofit Center and President, Nonprofit Management Association*

2. The nature of the work suggests the need for more than one person

Some consulting projects require more than one kind of expertise and require the use of two or more consultants.

When working on a complex, emotion-laden assignment such as mediating staff conflict or resolving an organizational crisis, a team of consultants can provide support for one another. They can also help maintain objectivity, or share the burden if they're being "dumped on."

The nature of such work might be intense, such as consulting with a large group or through a long session. In this case, team consulting gives an opportunity to break the monotony of a single facilitator or presenter for the participants—and it also gives the consultants a break.

You may want to team when you're working with an organization or community group with many subparts. Different consultants can take responsibility for different subparts of the overall system. For example, one might work with the administrative staff and one with program staff; or one on marketing and one on finance.

I often use a consulting team when planning an extended meeting for a large group of people, like a neighborhood visioning session or a planning meeting with a large collaborative. In these situations the event might call for the use of a cadre of small-group facilitators to work with me at the event and possibly for a while afterward in follow-up work. In this situation, a consulting team is developed for short-term use during the project. The lead consultant's responsibility is to provide the consulting team members with adequate orientation and training so they can do their jobs well for the event or assignment.

In some cases you may need to create an "internal-external" team. Some projects call for an internal contact person who can be a focus for communication and who already knows the organization or system. The internal person not only manages the project communications but also ensures continuity after the consulting project is done. Or, the organization may have someone already in the position of training director or planner—someone who typically does the work the consultant is being called in for. You might also team with an internal to train her or him in a new skill.

3. More than one person would be more efficient

Teaming can also be done for efficiency's sake. For example, in a large data gathering project, where a number of interviews need to be done in a short time, consultants can split up the tasks and do them simultaneously. Or if an organization is anxious to move through a large project quickly, two or more consultants might divide up the work to meet their deadlines. On occasion it saves time to bring in another consultant who has a lot of experience with a particular task, thereby reducing the amount of time the primary consultant needs to spend learning to do that task. You may also want other consultants, researchers, or support people doing work that calls for different levels of expertise.

4. Training or development of one of the consultants is needed

Team consulting is an excellent way to mentor beginning consultants or to work with someone to enhance your own development. The "senior" consultant can coach and model behaviors and skills, and the "apprentice" can either observe or participate in some capacity during the project. Often consultants, when faced with a portion of a large project that is unfamiliar to them, might bring in a more experienced consultant just to coach them through that one piece. In some cases the client doesn't even know this is happening—it can be done behind the scenes.

Team Consulting May Be Inappropriate When . . .

1. It requires too much cost or support from the client

Working as a team always needs to be negotiated up front with the client if it's going to result in additional cost to them—either monetarily or in tying up staff time. The lead consultant needs to discuss the pros and cons with the client—what benefit the additional consultant would offer, and what other options might be.

2. The number of consultants becomes top-heavy or overpowering for the client

Never outpower your client; in fact, hesitate to "equal" your client. This relates to both number of people and the psychological impact that you have in an organization. Consultants, just by the nature of their role, bring a powerful dynamic into a group. If the client isn't experienced with consultants or naturally holds consultants in awe, the impact of a second consultant might be overwhelming. If you are meeting with one person in the client setting and hope to talk frankly about difficult issues, be cautious about bringing one or more other consultants with you. The imbalance in numbers may inhibit your client's disclosures.

3. Adding a second consultant may put too much distance between the client and consultant

Adding a second consultant tends to formalize the client-consultant relationship. With one consultant, there's a personal connection between the consultant and the representatives of the client group. This personal connection might make it easier, in some cases, for the client to ask for help or share frustrations. A second consultant changes the dynamics. At some times the client relates to one consultant; at other times the other. Or one member or group in the client system relates to one consultant and another person or group to another person. There is no one person who knows all the pieces, and trust is more diffused.

You can see there are many advantages to team consulting, including that for the consultant it's often a whole lot more fun to work with a partner. But the decision to work in a team needs to be made with the needs of the client coming first, and in direct consultation with the client.

Challenges in Team Consulting

1. Changing lead consultants in midstream

I've never worked on a consulting project that went well where there was a change in lead consultants midway through a project. Sometimes it's necessary to change lead consultants because of changes in the focus of the work, or changes in personal circumstances (such as availability or personal demands). Whenever that has happened, however well I've tried to manage it, the quality of the overall consultation has suffered. The new lead consultant almost has to start over in establishing a relationship and clarifying the work to be done.

2. Working in teams created by someone else

Often a client will piece together a consulting team, hiring one person to do research, one person to do facilitation, and another person to work with a particular group. They expect that these consultants will coordinate their work. Pulling the consultants together to talk about each of their respective roles and outcomes and how the pieces fit together will help integrate the work. Hopefully there is enough chemistry among the consultants to work together well; if the chemistry is missing, it will take diligent attention to communications and role clarification, and ongoing negotiation of the intersection points of the different consultants' work.

I have had a couple of experiences working on projects with other consultants that haven't gone well. Through these experiences I've learned the importance of having a clear contract with the other consultant that outlines who is responsible for what. Then, if someone blows it, it is easy to figure out what is going wrong and how to fix it. I once helped a successful fund-raising consultant, whom I had known for twenty years, with a capital campaign for a large organization. The client started calling me because they weren't getting information from the first consultant, who was going through a messy divorce. He was missing deadlines and not showing up for meetings. I ended up holding the bag for someone who wasn't delivering. Eventually the client canceled the contract, and I had to pick up the pieces and close out the contract. Now I think twice about being co-consultant with a friend, because if it goes wrong, I may have to choose between friendship and a work relationship.

— *Barbara Davis*
Independent Consultant

Internal vs. External Consulting

Few organizations in the nonprofit sector are large or well-financed enough to have internal consulting staff. The exceptions include some of the larger, national-scope organizations, such as the Girl Scouts, the American Lung Association, the Red Cross, some larger-city United Ways, and government agencies. These larger organizations may have people on their staff (such as human resources specialists, training directors, planners, and communications directors) whose responsibilities in part might be providing consultation internally to different parts of the organization.

You may, however, work in an organization where you are asked occasionally to take on a project or serve as facilitator. Although you don't have a formal title of consultant, often the work you are asked to do is outside of your normal job responsibilities and in many ways resembles consulting (that is, you take on a role of providing assistance to a person, group, organization, or community wanting to build their capacity, accomplish a task, or achieve a goal). For the purpose of this occasional assignment, you in effect become an internal consultant.

Consulting from an internal position has many similarities with external consulting—and some key differences. The process of consulting is the same. The stages of the consulting process are relevant and appropriate from either an external or internal position. Internal consulting requires the same set of skills, and likewise demands a broad repertoire of consulting roles. Finally, some internal consultants, like external ones, even charge fees for their time to other departments within the organization.

The main difference between internal and external consulting is that as an internal consultant, your relationship with the client is not temporary. The internal consultant usually has a salaried, long-term relationship with the organization. And the internal consultant's clients are often on a peer level or even above them in the hierarchy of the organization. One of the issues, then, is that the internal consultant has a lot at stake in taking on a project. It's often difficult for an internal consultant to be frank and challenging, to give difficult feedback, or to be the bearer of bad tidings, because the consultant's paycheck depends on the organization's support. A second difficulty is that as a member of the organization, it's tough for an internal consultant to be objective. The internal consultant often already has opinions about most things that are going on in the organization, whether it's people's skills or the strategic direction of the organization. Managing these personal opinions and judgments and trying to provide objective counsel can be difficult.

Internal consulting is especially difficult when it is only part of a person's job responsibilities. When a staff member has a full-time assignment to be a consultant to different departments or programs, it's easier to maintain an image and self-concept of separateness or objectivity from the daily workings of the organization. When that's not the case, you might want to consider these guidelines, to help you keep a constructive relationship with your internal clients:

1. Always develop a clear written contract with each client

Formalize the relationship, even if it is only a one-page memo in which you outline what the consulting objectives are, what the steps will be, and who has responsibility for what. Pay particular attention to relationship issues (see Chapter 2) and agreements about feedback, confidentiality, and reporting. Discuss the implications of your employee relationship with the client and address any issues or concerns that either the client or you might have.

2. Be clear about what skills you have and don't have

Internal consultants who are good often get called in to do everything and anything that needs to be done, even tasks with which they have no experience. Watch that you don't get in over your head or make commitments that you can't follow through on.

3. Be clear about termination of the consulting work

As you are clear and formal about the beginning of a consulting project, be clear and formal about the ending. Don't let the consulting relationship on one project spill over into other areas of your work relationship.

4. Gracefully decline projects that might be inappropriate for you to accept

Internal consultants often know many people in the groups with which they consult. Relationships that are particularly prone to conflict of interest include being a member of the part of the organization that needs consulting assistance, being in a supervisory relationship with anyone in the group, or having a personal friendship with someone in the group . If you feel that you will temper your advice, not challenge a decision, or not be objective because of organizational relationships, the consulting project may not be appropriate for you. Whether a project poses a conflict of interest has to be determined case by case by the consultant and the client. Facilitating a planning meeting might pose no problem; doing an organization assessment and interviewing other staff in the group might well strain your objectivity. You can always refer the client to two or three other resources from outside the organization.

Ethical Issues in Consultation

Every kind of work we do involves ethical dilemmas and choices. Because of the enormous power we have in organizations and groups, consultants are especially prone to questions of what is right, appropriate, or ethical, not only with our own choices and behavior but also in reaction to our clients. How we handle these situations can have great impact on our work and our relationship with our clients.

Consulting involves the deliberate assessment of and intervention in organizational and community life. This implies a commitment to influencing or changing organizational and interpersonal behaviors, policies, and practices. We are often hired because we are experts or can do something better than others. Because of this, every action and interaction on our part models best practice to the client. In effect, we are given the ability to influence others, even before we say anything.

In the absence of any universally established licensure or professional standards for consultants, each of us has to arrive at our own set of ethical standards. Appendix F, Nonprofit Management Association Professional Standards for Management Assistance Providers, on page 217, contains another set of ethical guidelines for management assistance providers. In this section I will share some ethical standards that have guided my work and suggest that an important development step for every consultant is exploring and articulating your own ethical positions related to your work.

The ethical positions that have guided my work include the following commitments:

1. **I try to ensure that my consulting practice meets the highest ethical, business, and interpersonal standards.**

   - I won't pressure clients to accept services or to continue with services that they no longer want—they must be free to choose, and I should be ready to step out.

   - My services will be priced fairly according to a market- or value-based rationale.

   - I will present all claims, recommendations, or data accurately and attribute sources appropriately.

   - When I am biased about a position or situation, I will claim that bias and offer to extricate myself from the situation.

   - I will acknowledge any and all real or possible conflicts of interest, including personal relationships with members of the group, before or during a consulting engagement.

2. **I try to stay aware of the influence I have, and not behave in exploitative ways or engage with clients in ways that have high potential for harm (for example, intellectually, sexually, physically, or emotionally).**

My words can influence feelings, behaviors, policies, and even the existence of the organization or group. My interventions can have both direct and indirect effects, often unanticipated. I try to use this power appropriately and help to empower members of the client system. I will get my own personal needs (for affiliation, recognition, power, or attention) met outside of the client relationship.

3. **I actively try to increase my self-awareness about, and skills in dealing with, behaviors and attitudes related to dehumanization and oppression.**

Organizations are fertile settings for deliberately or subtly inappropriate uses of power. I need to be clear about my own beliefs and abilities and to develop my own sensitivities and skills so that I am able to respond in a way that represents high standards of human regard and legal compliance.

4. **I work toward increased capacity and acknowledgment of strengths within the client system rather than focusing on client deficiencies or fostering dependence on the consultant or any external authority.**

The ideal consulting project ends with the client feeling like they solved the problem or accomplished the goal, and believing that they know how to, and can, address similar issues on their own in the future. To accomplish this I need to involve the client in all steps of the process, ensuring their participation and ownership of data and decisions.

5. **I represent honestly my experience and abilities and the services that I can provide and won't promise more than I can deliver.**

It's tempting to accept work that stretches my abilities or experience and that may lead me into new types of work, or into areas that are a little beyond my previous experience. The art is in knowing when to accept the work honestly, knowing I have the skills and expertise to do it well; when to tactfully tell the client I would like to do the work but it is slightly beyond my experience (and then jointly make the decision with the client whether to take it on); and when to decline an engagement.

6. **I protect the rights of originators of creative materials.**

I try to be rigorous in respecting copyrights and sources and crediting originators of theory, examples of practice, or tools or instruments borrowed or adapted for a client.

7. **I honor commitments of confidentiality or anonymity.**

   When I make a commitment of confidentiality or anonymity I honor that commitment to the extent that I can under the law. I don't disclose the names of, or information about, clients without their permission.

8. **I try to ensure the rights of all members of a client system, rather than supporting some at the expense of others.**

   I attempt to pay attention to all parts of the client system and to be attentive to how decisions or changes are affecting individuals and different parts of the system. It is natural to be more attracted to some people or groups than others, to understand one point of view and even agree with it more than with others. The challenge is to represent the differences and help the client system find regard for and resolution of differences in goals, values, methods, or styles.

Chapter Three Summary

In this chapter we looked at five aspects of consultation that enhance our effectiveness and add variety and artistry to what we do:

- Consulting roles
- Facilitating change
- Team consulting
- Internal vs. external consulting
- Consulting ethics

We learned that we need to carefully adapt what we do to the unique needs of the organizations or groups with which we work. It's important to understand the dynamics of the systems in which we work, and we need to pay particular attention to our own choices and behavior which will, whether we're aware of it or not, have a powerful impact on the client. We explored the choice of working solo or as a team, and looked at the unique dynamics of being an internal consultant.

The next chapter focuses on building and managing our consulting practice—the nuts and bolts of our profession.

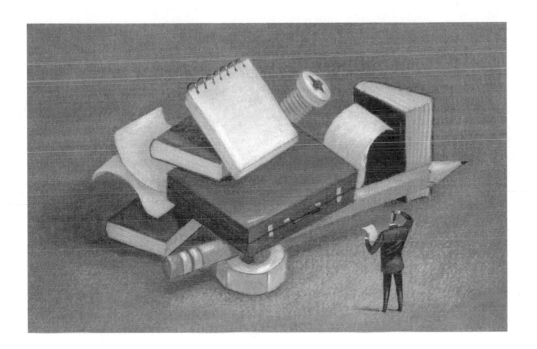

CHAPTER FOUR

Nuts and Bolts

Managing Your Consulting Practice

In the previous three chapters we've discussed the nonprofit sector, different kinds of consulting, the process of consulting, and consulting roles. These chapters gave you a grounding in the basics of consulting and provided information on adapting your skills and your practice to a number of unique situations and cultures you will encounter while consulting.

But a big part of the work of consulting is away from your clients. To sustain your practice over time you need to manage your practice as a business. Like any small business, the most successful consultants study their environment and markets, assess their capabilities and weaknesses, develop plans for what they hope to accomplish and how they will get there, and implement their plans. And they do this kind of business planning on a regular basis, constantly learning about their markets and refining their goals and strategies.

Many excellent books are available on business planning for consultants (see Appendix A: Resources, on page 163, for a few suggestions). These books offer in-depth coverage of the many aspects of business planning for a consulting practice. This chapter, which is intended as an overview, will highlight six aspects of business planning and managing a consulting practice that are essential for both beginning and experienced consultants.

The six elements are:

- Marketing your services
- Establishing consulting rates
- Estimating project costs
- Evaluating consulting services
- Managing your development as a consultant
- Funding consultation and technical assistance

Marketing Your Services

I described the beginning of the consulting process in Stage 1 as getting a call from a prospective client. If only each week would start with getting a new inquiry! Some consultants with well-established reputations do get more calls than they can handle. But that enviable position results from years of establishing a reputation, a track record of excellent work, and a large network of relationships. Many consultants with booming business say that they never "do marketing." So what is the magic formula for being successful and having a steady stream of the right kind of business?

Those consultants, consulting groups, or management support organizations with more demand than capacity probably don't have to sell their services at all. They may not even be aware that what they are doing is really marketing at its best—doing high-quality work, maintaining strong relationships with past and current clients, pursuing opportunities to do new and challenging work, continually learning and meeting people.

Marketing has been defined as a process that helps you exchange something of value for something you need. The marketing process involves establishing exchange relationships that are mutually beneficial[16]. Marketing helps you to establish the kind of practice you want, receive the rewards or remuneration that you need, and at the same time contribute your skills and expertise to benefit your clients.

The following five steps will help you develop a marketing plan for your consulting practice. These steps will work for you whether you are an independent consultant, a part-time volunteer, or part of a management support organization.

---

[16] Stern, Gary J., *Marketing Workbook for Nonprofit Organizations* (Saint Paul, Minn.: Wilder Publishing Center, 1990).

1. Create a vision for your practice

2. Assess the feasibility of achieving that vision

3. Clarify your marketing goals

4. Develop strategies to achieve your goals

5. Work your plan

As you work through these steps, you will learn how to embed a marketing mentality into your day-to-day work. Rather than something you do two days a week, marketing will become a part of how you do business on a day-to-day basis. In Appendix D, Consultant Worksheets, you will find Worksheet 8 on page 205, Develop a Marketing Plan for Your Consultation Business, which you can use to work through this process in detail.

1. Create a vision for your practice

To create a personal vision of the kind of work you hope to do and the kind of impact you want to have, ask yourself the following questions: What kind of practice do you want? What services or products do you want to provide your clients? Who will your clients be? What client characteristics—values, culture, style—are especially important to you? Where are you consulting—locally, nationally, internationally? Will you be working alone or with other consultants? How much time will you devote to your work? How would you like people to describe you and your work? Here is a sample vision for a consulting practice:

> In three years I am a recognized and respected consultant assisting local nonprofit organizations of all types with strategic positioning and alignment. My work is instrumental in helping nonprofits become flexible in responding to rapidly changing trends in their communities and proactive in creating opportunities for extending their impact. My ideal client is open to new ideas and feedback and is actively seeking new ways of doing business. My client relationships are longer term, usually beginning with a planning effort and evolving into an intermittent coaching role interspersed with occasional more intense interventions. I have an independent practice but am closely connected with a web of other consultants with whom I occasionally team on projects and exchange referrals. I meet regularly with these consultants to share ideas, learn, and do joint marketing. Most of my work comes from referrals from satisfied past clients.

Write your vision down and keep it in front of you, literally. Tape it to your computer or the wall above your desk. A clearly stated and heartfelt vision will help you recognize opportunities, make choices, communicate your hopes and values, and move steadily toward your goals.

2. Assess the feasibility of achieving that vision

You have some homework to do to determine whether your vision is achievable, and where you need to focus your efforts to make it happen. To determine the feasibility of creating your ideal practice, analyze your market *and* your capabilities. You can determine whether your vision is attainable by answering the following questions:

Regarding market

- *Who are your potential clients?* List categories of potential clients and identify (or at least count) organizations within those categories to determine how large your potential market is.

- *What are your potential clients' challenges, needs, and wants?* Do these fit with the kind of work you want to do? You can get this information by gathering it on your own (an effective marketing strategy) or obtaining it through other sources who study nonprofits such as state associations of nonprofits, United Ways, and foundations.

- *Who else is doing this work?* Are they potential allies or partners? Is the market saturated with consultants doing this work? Or are there few other resources in this field? Contact other consultants to learn what they are doing or if there are local or national networks of consultants in your field. Some resources are listed in Appendix A, Resources, on page 177.

Regarding capabilities

- *Do you have the skills, expertise, and credentials to do this work?* This may be difficult to determine. There are no general certification organizations for nonprofit consultants unless you are in a field that requires it, such as accounting. See Worksheet 5 in Appendix D, Consultant Worksheets, page 197, for a beginning list of general nonprofit consulting competencies that you can use for self-assessment.

- *What would a potential client expect a consultant to have in training, experience, and credentials?* Head back to the streets. You'll have to find this out on your own for your field and geographic area.

- *Given the two previous questions, do you have the required and expected skills, experience, and credentials?* What additional training, experience, or credentials do you need to acquire to do this work well? How can you obtain those? This is the time for frank, honest self-assessment. A lot can be learned through experience, but the best consultants have a base of solid training that gives them expertise in a particular area.

3. Clarify your marketing goals

What is it you are trying to accomplish? Are you hoping to establish, or change, your reputation in the field? Do you want to expand your practice, or scale back? Do you need to enhance your credentials for doing this work? Are you hoping to change your geographic reach or work in a different nonprofit industry? Do you want to work with other consultants or a management support organization?

The marketing strategies you select will be different if you want to establish a full-time independent national practice, get occasional consulting contracts with local organizations for a side income, or become part of a management support organization to gain experience and get your name known. If you are already part of a management support organization, you may be wanting to expand into a new line of business, or work more with a different kind of client. Take the time to define thoughtful short- and long-term marketing goals for your consulting practice.

> I work through an informal association of four independent consultants. It is like a "virtual consulting business." We don't maintain an office or have paid staff. We work out of our home offices. We market our services together and have a common brochure. We offer the client better services because each of us has different specialized expertise—one is a fiscal wizard, one does grant writing, one knows PR, one does strategic planning. It takes the pressure off of trying to keep up with everything. I don't feel so guilty about the tall stack of unread articles in my office. If I need to know something I can ask the others. It's an interesting way of solving the isolation issues that independent consultants face—and provides a lot of moral support for all of us.
>
> — *Diane Brown*
> *Non-Profit Assistance Group*

4. Develop strategies to achieve your goals

Identify strategies and action steps that will help you achieve your marketing goals. Keep in mind what you learned and need to learn from the feasibility analysis about your market and capabilities. Pay attention to both short- and long-term strategies that will help guide the development of your practice.

There are generally two categories of strategies: reputation building and relationship building. Most consultants will pay attention to both kinds of strategies on an ongoing basis. If you are just starting out you will definitely need to work on both kinds of strategies. If you have an established reputation but your relationships or networks are weak or you want to expand your market, focus on relationship-building strategies. If you have strong networks and relationships but your experience and reputation as a nonprofit consultant are weak, or you want to expand your expertise, focus on reputation-building strategies.

Nonprofits are becoming more sophisticated about using consultants. Fifteen years ago, people imported consultants from the city into our rural area. Consultants brought models and styles that worked in the urban setting but didn't work here. When we started (fifteen years ago), we had to do a lot of education. We had to hold clients' hands, dispel myths about consultants, and restore confidence after bad experiences. People were almost allergic to consultants. That's turning around. Now organizations in rural areas know more about using consultants. But it has taken time, and careful tending to relationships.

— *Diane Brown*
Non-Profit Assistance Group

Following are some suggested strategies to consider. These suggestions are a starting point. Be creative in generating your own ideas.

Reputation-Building Strategies

1. Produce work of such quality and value that the work speaks for itself, and others are motivated to use you. Most successful consultants get the majority of their work from referrals and repeat clients.

2. Create and publish products, articles, books. Contribute to nonprofit newsletters and publications, as well as professional publications, locally and nationally.

3. Offer to donate training or consulting services to help you refine your approach or tools and gain experience.

4. Team up with established consultants to gain experience. These consultants can also become referral sources in the future.

5. Write summaries of what you are learning in a particular area of your work, and send it to select organizations, asking for their feedback.

6. Become an expert in an area that is cutting edge or in high demand.

7. Develop promotional materials: client list, résumé, vita, business card, brochure, or service descriptions.

8. Research local or national nonprofit associations and submit proposals to do conference presentations in your area of expertise. The Internet is full of information on nonprofits and associations.

9. Follow up on every opportunity you hear about to do work that is aligned with your interests and values.

10. Obtain additional training or education to better prepare you to do the work you want to do. Ask experienced people already doing that work what they recommend as preparation.

Relationship-Building Strategies

1. Always send thank-you letters to clients and referral sources.

2. Call past clients three or six months after completion of a project to check in and see how they are doing with their implementation or follow-up steps. If they plan to have a follow-up session, ask if they would like you to assist them with it.

3. Follow up each lead and referral diligently.

4. Invest time in prospect development. Make a list of the twenty most desirable organizations that you would like to work with. Study them. Interview people to learn more about their successes and challenges. Volunteer to help them with one of their most pressing issues.

5. Send past or prospective clients articles related to their interests.

6. Establish referral networks, relationships with groups or organizations that will pass your name on to people needing assistance (for example, management support organizations, United Ways, or well-established nonprofit consultants.

7. Research the gatekeepers or leaders in a particular nonprofit industry and meet with them to learn what the trends and challenges are.

8. Serve on the board of a nonprofit.

9. Become active with the board or committees of a professional association such as the National Alliance for Nonprofit Management (NANM), American Society for Training and Development (ASTD), American Management Association (AMA), or others in your local community or field.

10. Attend workshops and conferences and network fiercely.

5. Work your plan

You've clarified what you want, determined how feasible that is, and what you need to do to get there. Don't put the plan on the shelf to gather dust. Your marketing plan needs to become a part of your everyday life, in your awareness every time you attend a meeting, read the newspaper, or talk to a client. You need a marketing mentality. Decide what you will do daily, weekly, or monthly and set up a reminder system so you don't let it slide. You may be amazed at what happens when you have a firm vision of where you want to be and begin creating opportunities to realize that vision.

Marketing Challenges

- ### *Aligning your work and values*

  When you are doing work which is aligned with your values, strengths, and interests, and your primary focus is on serving clients and helping them accomplish a worthwhile goal, energy is released. Athletes describe it as "the flow." When your values, goals, and practice are in alignment, you have fun. It doesn't even feel like work. You attract people, and business comes your way. Once you experience that alignment you will be hooked, and you will easily recognize its absence. Absence of that energy means that something is out of kilter—you aren't doing the kind of work you love, you aren't focused on serving the client, the chemistry with the client is missing, or something is preventing you from doing your best work. Pay attention to your energy.

I try to work in a way that is consistent with my values and beliefs. I don't see my consulting role as an outsider going in and out of groups. I am in long-term relationships with the folks who pay me. Their economic health and effectiveness affect me and my children. Recently, I was asked to work, for one day, with staff of a Native museum to deal with some problems they were having related to racism. I told them that I wouldn't consider doing the work unless we had an ongoing relationship, that one day wasn't enough to address their issues. We needed to probe reasons for their problems with the community. I encouraged the museum's education director to join a more broad-based dialogue on racial tensions that was already underway in the community. I made this recommendation because, to me, the troubles at the museum were just a microcosm of the problems in the larger community. The museum wasn't ready to make that commitment. Although I turned down the consulting job and didn't make any money, I still feel I made the best decision for the whole community and therefore for myself. Since that time, the museum's director, board members, and even the front desk clerk have had a change of heart and have engaged in the ongoing dialogue at no cost to them—and to the benefit of us all.

— *Ruth Yellow Hawk*
Independent Consultant

- ### *Thinking long term*

  There is a tremendous time lag between awareness and response in marketing. If you become aware that all your current contracts will end in two months, it's too late to drum up business to start at that time. Often the time span between a first discussion with a prospective client and finalizing a contract can be months or even a year. If you are looking at a major shift—change in services, expansion to a different part of the country, or scaling back to part time, you need to be thinking two to three years out. Marketing is an ongoing process and needs to be a part of your thinking every day. But keep your long-range goals in mind, and keep working toward them.

- ***Keeping in touch during busy times***

  At times we get very busy. It seems like we will never get a break. Everyone wants a report this week. It's easy, and a mistake, to neglect basic relationship-building strategies during these times. Make sure you make time for simple thank-you letters to referral sources and clients, and follow-up calls to past clients, even when you are busy. Maintaining these relationships will pay off in the long term.

  Whenever I go through a drought, eventually things open up. The slow periods are short-lived, and I've learned that they are a time to regroup and read, learn, be with my family, and reconnect with people. I also use this time to rethink what I want to do, not just respond to projects that come my way. I have a couple of long-term anchor relationships, and during slow periods I can increase the work I do for them. Other projects take cultivating. A useful tool for me has been to think about writing a book. The book projects never get completed, but the process of getting going on them leads to some work I really want to do. Once I proposed a series of books to be done with a colleague, set up some next steps to get going on the books, and in moving on those next steps got into some really interesting consulting work. The series of books never materialized. In fact, I've never written a book. But the process is useful for me. I've learned to trust the process, knowing that there will be work.

  — *Pixie Martin*
  Independent Consultant

- ***Balancing reality with dreams***

  Keep the vision of your ideal practice in front of you, and grab opportunities that have the potential to move you toward it. Be willing to step back from your ideal and take work occasionally to build relationships, gain experience and credentials (and pay the bills), but be sure you don't get stuck doing a kind of work that is not part of your ideal practice.

On Giving and Receiving

Some consultants look for ways they can give back to their clients, either through donations, a little volunteer work, or an occasional reduction in fees. In other cases the consultant is faced with the question of how much to receive. Performing arts organizations might offer complimentary tickets to performances, or a nonprofit might invite you to their fifty-dollar-a-plate annual dinner at no cost, or repeatedly offer to pick up your lunch tab. Nonprofit consultants commonly resolve this dilemma by accepting gifts that are necessary for their work (attending one performance may give you insight into artistic quality or customer service), but decline or offer to pay for gifts that don't serve that purpose.

Establishing Consulting Rates

Some consultants, especially those who are living on a retirement income or consulting as a sideline to assist a favorite organization, work on a volunteer basis and aren't interested in being reimbursed for their time or expenses. However, the majority of consultants need to earn a living. Determining the fee you will charge and costing out a project can be one of the most difficult aspects of starting a new consulting project.

How much should you charge? Unfortunately, I can't tell you what you should charge, or what the "going rate" is for what you do. You'll have to arrive at that decision yourself. This section will outline the various factors that you need to consider as you arrive at that decision, including:

- The type of consulting you do (writing, fund-raising, research, facilitation)

- What region you are working in (East Coast, Midwest, urban, rural)

- What industry you work in (child care, housing, education, arts)

- What the going rate is for consultants doing your kind of work

- How much competition there is for your kind of consulting

- How much experience you have

- Whether you expect consulting to be your only means of support or if it is supplemental income

- How quickly the client needs help, and how much that timing may inconvenience you or cause additional support expenses

Consulting rates in the nonprofit/community sector vary widely, typically ranging between $25 and $200 per hour (1998 dollars). Your best sources of information about the going rate in your field and community are other consultants or potential clients. But you need to make your own calculations.

There is a big difference between what you charge and what your net income is. One approach is to think about what you should charge as a consultant compared to what you might make doing similar work in a salaried position. If the salary is $50,000 or roughly $25 per hour, multiply that by a factor of three to four to build in all of your taxes, overhead, benefits, and unbillable hours (marketing, project start-up, sick days, vacation, administration). This would result in a consulting rate of $75 to $100 per hour. Another method is to assume that your income will be approximately two-thirds of your gross billables, factoring in taxes, benefits, and a minimal level of overhead (but excluding direct project costs). So if you bill $100,000 per year, your net earnings will be approximately $67,000.

Some additional considerations when thinking about what to charge are the going rate in your region, the position you want to establish in the marketplace, the cost of operations, the demand for your type of services, sliding fee scales, and your personal values.

- *Going rate:* Find out what the going rate is for your type of work. What do competitors charge for the same kind of work with the same kind of organizations?

- *Positioning:* How do you want to position yourself in relation to the market? What do other consultants doing similar work in the same area charge for their services? Can you, and do you want to, compete with the top people in your field, with a high rate? Are you just starting out, with little experience? If many people are doing your kind of consulting, you will need to find a unique niche or resign yourself to compete with the pack. Consider charging a lower rate when you are learning a new kind of service to get experience.

- *Cost of operations:* What does it cost you to deliver an hour of service? You need to decide which expenses to absorb as overhead and build into your hourly or per diem rate, and which you will bill separately for in your project budgets. Figure 13 on page 148 shows typical overhead and project costs.

- *Demand:* What are your clients willing to pay? Will your clients perceive enough value added to pay what you want to charge? Do they have a budget or ceiling for the consulting project? Note that value is related to your reputation, position, and niche, and the results that you can deliver. There is a higher perceived value if you have a strong reputation, a lot of experience, or the service you offer is unique. There is a lower perceived value if you don't have a long list of past client references, or if there are numerous people who are doing what you do.

- *Sliding fee scales:* Sliding fee scales are more common in the non-profit sector than in the for-profit and public sectors. Consultants will sometimes charge less for organizations with lower budgets (for example, under $250,000) or organizations that are in their neighborhood or city.

- *Personal values:* Some consultants have strong values that influence the fees they charge. Values can be related to economic realities of the nonprofit sector or a sense of social responsibility or economic justice, and can result in rates policies such as charging no more than the hourly salary of the highest-paid person in the organization, or charging an organization that serves people under the poverty line a lower rate.

If you are just starting out as a consultant you may have a difficult time determining what you should charge. You might even be shocked at the rates many consultants charge, and have difficulty asking for that level of fee. I often tell consultants to decide what they need to charge, taking into account all of the mentioned factors, and then practice telling what your rate is to a friend or in front of a mirror, so you can do it with confidence and a straight face.

Figure 13   *Cost of Operations*

Typical Overhead Costs

office space, utilities, maintenance

telephone

Internet access and charges

equipment purchase or rental: computers, printer, fax, copier, phones, flip charts, tape recorders, overhead projectors, office furniture

administrative time: correspondence, billing, record keeping, evaluation

marketing: meetings, meals, promotional materials, research

development: subscriptions, conference fees, books

taxes

insurance and other benefits

sick and vacation time

secretarial support

retirement

office supplies

equipment maintenance

tax and bookkeeping assistance

postage, courier, and delivery costs

Typical Project Costs

proposal writing

prep time

delivery time

travel time and costs

room and board

materials design, illustration, and production

copying and printing

project assistance: research, data entry, interviewers, other consultants

meeting space rental, food, supplies

Estimating Project Costs

I've never known a consultant who hasn't at one time or another seriously underestimated the time it would take to complete a project. It must be a rite of passage as a consultant to take a bath, so to speak, on a project. Estimating costs is difficult without a lot of experience, and without knowing the client and how they work. It would be easy if you could just say "I charge x dollars per hour and I'll bill you for actual time." But few clients are comfortable with that arrangement; most have a budget or want a ceiling, if not a fixed price, for the work.

The key to estimating project costs accurately is found in the first stage of the consulting process. The proposal format that we outlined included a step-by-step work plan, and a delineation of responsibilities between you and the client. These two elements of the proposal are your building blocks for estimating cost. The more detail you've built into the work plan and the better you are at anticipating some of the hidden time (such as phone calls, thinking time, letter writing, revisions, unanticipated meetings), the more accurate your estimates will be.

The process of estimating expenses other than time is more difficult to generalize as it varies widely with the kind of consulting you are doing. Figure 13 (Cost of Operations) will give you an idea of the kind of project expenses you might encounter. Some consultants will estimate time and direct project expenses, and then add on a percentage such as 15 or 20 percent to cover overhead and unanticipated expenses.

Figure 14, Sample Consulting Project Budget Worksheet (page 150), shows a sample project budget worksheet that can be used in tandem with your proposal to estimate costs. In Appendix D, Consultant Worksheets, on page 211, you will find Worksheet 9, a blank version of this figure that you can copy and use as needed.

Billing Methods

Once you have calculated the time and expenses for your project, you have to decide how you want to bill the client. Five billing methods are used most often in the nonprofit sector:

1. *Fee per unit of time:* You charge an hourly rate or a per diem (daily) rate.

2. *Fee per unit of time with a not-to-exceed ceiling:* This is the same as number 1 above, but you stipulate a maximum amount that you will bill and guarantee to complete the work within that amount.

Figure 14	Sample Consulting Project Budget Worksheet

Budget assumptions:

1. Consultant time will be billed at $75/hour. Billable consultant time includes meeting preparation, meetings, report writing, planning sessions, and travel time.

2. Administrative support time will be billed at $25/hour for data entry; all other support time will be nonbillable.

Cost estimates:

Step (from proposal work plan)	Hours	Fee	Expenses	Total Cost
1. Get agreement on project objectives, work plan, and budget. Meetings with board chair and executive committee.	4	$300		$300
2. Orient consultant to organization's history and plans.	3	225		225
3. Decide data collection strategy and audience: two planning committee meetings.	12	900		900
4. Design focus group questions; test and finalize.	5	375		375
5. Conduct three focus groups and five interviews.	18	1,350	$300	1,650
6. Summarize results. (Support staff)	4	100		100
7. Write summary report. Review with client; revise as needed.	10	750		750
8. Produce ten copies of report. (Support staff)	2	40	60	100
9. Present report at board meeting.	4	300		300
TOTALS	**62**	**$4,340**	**$360**	**$4,700**

3. *Flat fee:* You estimate your cost and then give the client a flat rate for the work, regardless of how long it takes. If you go over the fee, you eat the difference. If you come in under your estimate, you keep the extra.

4. *Retainer fee:* Used most often to level out the consultant costs on a long-term, usually large project, the retainer establishes a monthly payment level that is usually reconciled with actuals at the project end.

5. *Lump sum payments:* With larger organizations, or larger projects, an arrangement may be set up to charge a minimum amount at the beginning of a project to cover out-of-pocket expenses, and then charge the balance upon receipt of the "deliverables" (reports or other products). Or you might bill the total cost in three or four installments.

The billing method you use should be written into any proposals or contracts you negotiate with your clients. Ideally this will be discussed and agreed on in advance to ensure that it meets both of your needs and there is no confusion once the project starts.

Evaluating Consulting Services

The purpose of evaluating your consulting services is twofold:

1. To determine whether you have accomplished the consulting objectives to the client's satisfaction

2. To learn what you can about improving your consulting practice for the future

In Stage 6 of the consulting process we discussed how, as part of reaching closure with the client on the project, you can ask for feedback on your services. We noted that this can be done formally or informally, through a brief conversation, a discussion with the whole group you worked with, or through a written evaluation form. Evaluation forms are most useful when you want to get feedback from more than one person in a client organization, such as the board chair and the executive director.

We have found that we can't wait until the end of a consultancy to assess effectiveness. We ask consultants to do this informally throughout the process, and we also have an ongoing quality assurance process that has added greatly to the quality of our consultancies. At our consulting group, we have a quality assurance person who faxes and calls each client each month to check in on general satisfaction. These are brief phone calls, but they help us proactively find small glitches that, without those calls, could well turn into major blind spots on the part of the consultant. They also help us understand the overall anatomy of a consultancy, so that we can anticipate bumps in the consulting process and prepare newer consultants for what's ahead. If I were an independent consultant, I would hire someone to do this on my behalf. I find that when we hire independent consultants, there is a lot of feedback we would like to give some of them, but it is difficult to be straightforward with some who think extremely highly of themselves and who are not really open to feedback. An intermediary helps a lot.

— *Karen Simmons*
Director, LaSalle University Nonprofit Center and President, Nonprofit Management Association

I've included two different evaluation forms in this book, both created by Wilder Research Center as part of their ongoing evaluation of consulting services at the Amherst H. Wilder Foundation, where I work. These were designed for use with Wilder Foundation's Services to Organizations consulting group but could just as easily be adapted for use by an independent consultant. Evaluation forms can also be adapted to get feedback on more than one consultant if you are working as a team, to suit your particular line of work, or to select specific areas for feedback.

The two evaluation forms that I've included ask for different information. The first version focuses on the client's perception of overall quality of and satisfaction with the consultation, and the extent to which you performed commonly valued consulting behaviors. The second version asks for the client's assessment of the extent to which the consulting objectives were met, and asks for feedback on consulting quality in a different way from the first version. These forms, which may be reproduced or adapted for your consulting practice, are found as Worksheets 6 and 7 in Appendix D, Consultant Worksheets, on page 201.

Managing Your Development as a Consultant

Most consultants I know crave development experiences and actively work at their own development. We will go to conferences, workshops, search conferences, forums, satellite conferences, readings, networking gatherings. We will take day classes, evening classes, play therapy classes. We go on vision quests and pore over catalogues for experiential wilderness learning experiences. We long to team with other consultants so we can learn from them. That is, we do these things when we have time. The problem is, we have little time, because we're always on our client's schedules.

It's really important to attend to your own training and ongoing development. I learned consulting by apprenticeship. Over the years training has been vitally important in helping me think through how I will approach a client situation. Keeping up with technology is an especially big challenge for retired consultants.

Many nonprofits are using technology to manage their human resources, data processing, and finance functions. It's especially hard, and vitally important, for retired people to keep on top of all these changes.

— *William P. Hall*
Volunteer Consultant, Executive Service
Corps of Chicago

So many people enter the consulting field with much less experience than they need. What consultants need is to see issues play out in a wide variety of organizations over time; awareness of what is going on in the people and the group, and the skills to be responsive to the group; a really big toolchest, so if an approach isn't working they can move to a different tool; strong facilitation skills; and the confidence to step back and put a process issue on the table for the group to deal with. Too

many consultants are rigid in their approach, and nonprofits stay polite and don't challenge a consulting approach that doesn't work. We need to figure out how to shorten the learning curve for consultants.

— *Patty Oertel*
President, Oertel Group and former
Executive Director, Southern California
Center for Nonprofit Management

I've learned how important it is to keep my own issues separate from the client's issues. I once worked on a consulting team with a woman, assisting a predominately female organization with restructuring. I was the only man in the room during one session when the client group started talking about male organizations and ways of doing things in a derogatory tone. I got into my head, thinking to myself, "How can I possibly help these women because I'm a white man. I'm no longer objective and can't serve them as a consultant." So I wound up taking myself out of the group. I abandoned my partner to resolve alone conflicted issues

about equity, race, and gender in the group. I was unable to focus on the client's issues and lost confidence in my own ability. The next day I had to step in and do some work with them alone, and I was able to put my issues aside and focus on what they needed. I've learned to notice my issues but not let them interfere with my ability, and to focus on what the client needs to be successful. I trust the client's decision to hire me because they believe I have something to offer them.

— *Emil Angelica*
Amherst H. Wilder Foundation

What I don't see consultants doing, especially those starting out as consultants, is acquiring basic training in various aspects of consultation. Nearly every consultant needs skills in interpersonal communications, conflict resolution, group facilitation, making presentations, business writing, project management, word processing, time management, and a host of others. These are competencies that are central to the consultant's role as intervenor in the lives of groups and organizations, central to our work in sustaining a consulting practice, and important for consultants regardless of their area of specialty.

I've organized basic and more advanced competencies by category as Worksheet 5, Core Competencies, so that you can use them for self-assessment and planning for your own development. You will find Worksheet 5 in Appendix D, Consultant Worksheets, on page 197.

There are many ways to develop skills and competencies. Attending a workshop or training session is the most obvious, and also the most expensive. Colleges and universities offer courses in many of these topics. Also check out some national organizations such as National Training Laboratories and University Associates. You can learn a lot through more informal means such as teaming up or apprenticing with an experienced consultant, reading, and volunteering to do work to learn.

Funding Consultation and Technical Assistance

Two inevitable parts of consulting in the nonprofit sector are helping clients find funding for consultation and managing relationships with the funders who support the nonprofits you serve. There are three main questions that nonprofit consultants have to deal with:

- How will your clients pay for your services?
- Should a funder be your client in assisting a nonprofit?
- What kind of relationships should you develop with funders?

Funding Consultation

A wise nonprofit will build consultation and technical assistance into their annual operating budget and view the expense as part of the cost of doing business. Given the current economic necessity of doing more with less, this strategy is not always successful. One of the first line items to be cut from a budget when times are tight is the cost of using outside consultants. The majority of organizations haven't budgeted for consulting costs and will have to be creative in finding the funds. Many nonprofits who find they need assistance end up looking for additional outside support to cover consulting costs. Many will ask the consultant for recommendations about how they might find these funds.

Nonprofit and community organizations receive money to support their work from several sources. The most common are fees, grants, contributions from donors and members, government contracts, and earned-income sources. Funders have an investment in the organizations they fund. They generally will do anything possible to help those organizations succeed. Most funders will see consultation as a legitimate expense in a funding proposal. Most funders will also consider an additional request from one of their grantees for a technical assistance grant, especially if it will cover a type of assistance that is central to their functioning and future survival. The funder may request that the organization obtain proposals from more than one consultant, or share the findings or products of the work with the funder at the conclusion of the work.

In some communities, private foundations, community foundations, or United Ways have set up creative mechanisms for making consulting and training assistance accessible to nonprofits. In some cases they have established pools of funds, or scholarship funds to support consulting, training, and technical assistance. These special funds are usually accessible more easily and quickly than traditional grant dollars. In other communities foundations directly support a management support organization that can then make its services available at low cost to nonprofit and community organizations.

Working with Funders

Both funders and consultants have the same desired outcome—to build the capacity of nonprofits so that they can have the greatest possible impact in the community. Funders are well-informed allies who support what you are doing. There is potential for establishing wonderful partnerships. There are some important ways that funders and consultants can work together to achieve this, and some situations that can be problematic. Following are five of these.

1. You will benefit greatly by educating yourself about the various funders in your area, their missions and funding priorities. This knowledge can be invaluable to your nonprofit clients. You can call funders and obtain annual reports and guidelines to learn about their priorities. Meeting with them is even better, but keep in mind that they are busy and have many demands on their time.

2. You will also likely meet representatives of foundations or United Ways in the course of your work. At times they sit on boards or committees that you work with; at other times you will need to interview them as part of data collection or getting feedback on a plan.

3. A common situation that can be difficult is when a funder, concerned about the viability of a grantee, decides to hire a consultant to assist the nonprofit—possibly to conduct an organizational assessment or to

develop a financial or strategic plan. They are, in essence, mandating consultation services as a condition of future funding. The funder in this situation intends to pay the consultant for his or her services and may want the consultant to report directly to them.

While this sounds like a good deal for the nonprofit, it doesn't always work that way. Since the nonprofit's future survival depends on the funder's support, they may feel uncomfortable openly sharing information about problems or challenges with the consultant. For the nonprofit to be fully engaged in their own development, it is important for the organization, funder, and consultant to be clear about who the consultant is working for and how information is to be shared.

A constructive arrangement in this kind of situation is for the non-profit and funder to sit down together and talk about what each of them hopes to get out of the consultation, the role the funder wants, and what kind of information the funder would like to receive at the end of the work. Sometimes the consultant is present; sometimes not. The funder then makes a grant directly to the nonprofit. The non-profit hires the consultant and the consultant gives all work and reports directly to the nonprofit. The nonprofit reports back to the funder as they agreed. This keeps the nonprofit in charge and ac-countable both for managing the consultant and for managing their own organization's development.

Some consulting projects are man-dated by funders. Quite a while ago I was working with a dance company. They had been told by a funder they had to do a strategic plan, and received a grant for the planning. It was clear when I met with them that the artistic director wanted to "get it over with"; his heart wasn't in it. The board displayed extreme reluctance about coming to meetings and making information available to me. It was like having a roomful of sullen teenagers. I finished the project, but the further along we got, the worse I felt. Looking back, if my radar had been more finely tuned, I might not have taken the job to begin with. But the second thing I learned was that once you're in a job and it begins to feel wrong, you're much better off to talk about it, to ask the client what's going on, or just say "this doesn't feel right" instead of soldiering on to the end. The dance company chose me as a consultant, I wasn't foisted on them, but they were dragging their heels and didn't want to do it. Now I would be inclined to ask, during intake, how can we structure the process so you can get something out of it that would be useful to you?

— *Barbara Davis*
Independent Consultant

I have learned to be very cautious in giving information about a client to a funder. Once I was called by a foundation that had funded an organization with which I was consulting. They asked how the organization was doing—whether they were financially sound. I responded ,"I know you're funding them, but my contract is with the organization you funded, so at the moment I am not able to communicate that information to you. You could ask them directly, or ask them if I could give you the information." The funder called the organization, and the executive director told me to feel free to communicate directly with the funder and tell them anything I wanted. I asked if he was concerned if I disclosed problems the organization was having. He said tell them anything. So I talked to the funder. When the funder asked about problems, I responded honestly. After that conversation, the director called and felt I had hurt his image with the funder. I talked to the director and went over everything I had said to the funder. It turned out that the funder got the damaging information from another source. But the situation raised a trust issue between me and the organization for future work. Since then, if a funder asks me questions about a client that require tough answers, I have a meeting or three-way phone conversation with the director and funder, or present the information in a letter that is approved by the director, in order to preserve trust with my client.

— *Emil Angelica*
Amherst H. Wilder Foundation

4. Funders also often hire nonprofit consultants to conduct grants reviews for potential grantees. If your primary practice is in one city or community and you regularly do grants review work for local funders, you may eventually limit your objectivity and availability for consulting with nonprofits supported by that funder. Your work with the funder will help you understand their standards and decision-making criteria and will give you information about the many organizations who apply for funding. The reverse is also true; if you regularly work with nonprofits, you may have biases, favorites, or special relationships that will limit your objectivity in doing objective grants review work. The nonprofit world in many communities is small, and if you have a local practice, you will, over time, develop a web of relationships with various funders and nonprofits. It is always wise to disclose prior relationships that may even slightly cause the perception of conflict of interest.

5. Occasionally potential funders of an organization will call you to ask for information about an organization with whom you've worked. I will generally, in this situation, refer the funder to the organization, or ask the client for permission before speaking about the organization.

Funders and consultants share a common goal, which is to see nonprofit and community groups excel in what they do. Work with funders to educate yourself and better support your nonprofit clients. But be sensitive to the unique relationship that funders and nonprofits have, and the complexity of becoming the third element in that relationship. When in doubt, talk about the relationship with your client and the funder.

Chapter Four Summary

In this chapter we have covered several topics related to managing your consulting practice, including:

- Marketing your services

- Establishing consulting rates

- Estimating project costs

- Evaluating consulting services

- Managing your development

- Funding consultation and technical assistance

These topics will help you build the foundation of a healthy, sustainable consulting practice and build your capacity for ongoing learning and development.

Managing an independent consulting business or a management support organization requires far more sophisticated management practices than what I've listed here. Setting up record-keeping and billing systems, obtaining insurance and appropriate technology, paying taxes, managing cash flow, and a myriad of other business management requirements need attention to manage your consulting practice well. Again I suggest you search out the many good resources available on business planning and small business management. Some of these are listed in Appendix A, Resources, on page 163.

Conclusion

The common stereotype is that anyone and everyone can become a consultant; if you know something you can consult. Consultant jokes abound. Because consulting is increasingly more common as a profession, the understanding of consulting as a process requiring both skill and artistry is becoming more important.

Consulting with nonprofit and community organizations adds another element to the definition of consulting. Nonprofit consultants tend to have a sense of mission about their work, as well as a deep commitment to doing work that contributes to the community. This book was written to support those people who share that commitment.

As I finish this book I'm struck with how much more there is to talk about. We've covered four big topics related to consulting with nonprofit and community groups: the environment; stages of the consulting process; consulting roles, dynamics, and ethics; and managing your consulting practice. And we've only danced across the surface of each one of those topics. Each topic could fill hours of conversation, and volumes of written material. That is exactly how I hope to leave you—hungry for more, and wanting to discuss and explore these topics further.

Appendices

APPENDIX A

Resources

Books and Articles

The following resources may be helpful for a variety of consulting situations. I have placed the following symbol 📖 next to those books I consider essential reading for the beginning consultant. Whenever possible, I have included the publisher's telephone number with the resource. In some cases, the publisher has changed or my personal copy is an older edition of a work that has been revised. For works specifically cited in footnotes or elsewhere in this text, I have named the publisher for the edition I own. For all other resources, I have attempted to list the publisher for the most recent edition available.

Andrews, Patricia Hayes, and John E. Baird, Jr. *Communication for Business and the Professions*. Dubuque, Iowa: Brown and Benchmark, 1995.

> *Presents communication strategies and skills necessary to handle interviews, group meetings, and public speeches.*

Angelica, Emil, and Vincent Hyman. *Coping with Cutbacks: The Nonprofit Guide to Success When Times Are Tight*. St. Paul, Minn.: Amherst H. Wilder Foundation, 1997.

> *Explains the changing relationship between the nonprofit and government sectors and offers a new way to think about resource problems in a nonprofit. Includes worksheets and six-step process for developing solutions to respond to shrinking resources.*

Barry, Bryan W. *Strategic Planning Workbook for Nonprofit Organizations, Revised and Updated.* St. Paul, Minn.: Amherst H. Wilder Foundation, 1997.

A guide to writing and implementing a strategic plan. Outlines five steps and provides worksheets to guide the planning process.

Beckhard, Richard. *Agent of Change: My Life, My Practice.* San Francisco, Calif.: Jossey-Bass, 1997. 415-433-1740.

Provides a history and theory of organizational change. Based on the author's professional memoirs as a pioneer in organizational development.

Bell, Chip, and Leonard Nadler. *Clients and Consultants: Meeting and Exceeding Expectations.* Houston, Tex.: Gulf Publishing, 1985.

Includes sections on developing client-consultant relationships, roles, compatibility, contracting, and frameworks.

Bellman, Geoffrey M. *The Consultant's Calling: Bringing Who You Are to What You Do.* San Francisco, Calif.: Jossey-Bass, 1990. 415-433-1740.

📖 *Describes consulting as a career, a living, and a life. Dissects the role of consultants.*

———. *Getting Things Done When You Are Not in Charge.* New York, N.Y.: Fireside, 1992.

Demonstrates how to lead, influence, and succeed from a supporting position.

———. *Making Consulting Valuable: How Clients and Consultants Can Gain the Most from Their Work Together.* Audiocassette. San Francisco, Calif.: Jossey-Bass, 1991. 415-433-1740.

Explores through conversations how qualities such as risk taking and leadership contribute to the successes and failures of consulting work.

Bermont, Hubert. *How to Become a Successful Consultant in Your Own Field.* Rocklin, Calif.: Prima Publishing, 1997. 916-632-4400.

Includes sections on gaining expertise, getting started, growing as a professional consultant, fees, contracts, proposals, reports, ethics, and competition in the consulting industry.

————. *The Successful Consultant's Guide to Writing Proposals and Reports*. Washington, D.C.: The Consultant's Library, 1979.

Analyzes reports and proposals as a unified whole. Describes the style, form, cover letter, organization, and format of a report and proposal. Demonstrates effective and ineffective reports and proposals.

Blake, Robert R., and Jane S. Mouton. *Consultation*. Reading, Mass.: Addison-Wesley, 1976.

📖 *Provides a model for diagnosing and intervening with organizations. Discusses theory and literature applicable to each consulting category. (A newer edition is available.)*

Block, Peter. *Flawless Consulting*. Austin, Tex.: Learning Concepts, 1981.

📖 *Uses illustrative examples, case studies, sample dialogues, and exercises to demonstrate ways of interacting with clients. (A newer edition is available.)*

Bobo, Kim, Jackie Kendall, and Steve Max. *Organizing for Social Change: A Manual for Activists in the 1990*, 2nd ed. Santa Ana, Calif.: Seven Locks, 1996.

Describes direct action organizing, obtaining fund-raising support, and methods for improving organizational skills.

Bridges, William. *Managing Transition*. Reading, Mass.: Addison-Wesley, 1991.

Describes the emotional impact of change on employees and what can be done to keep change from disrupting an entire organization. Provides practical techniques for bringing people on board with change.

Brinckerhoff, Peter C. *Mission-Based Management: Leading Your Not-for-Profit into the Twenty-First Century*. Dillon, Colo.: Alpine Guild, Inc., 1994. 800-869-9559.

📖 *Identifies the necessary skills for successful nonprofit leadership. Describes the ten biggest mistakes nonprofits make when planning for growth.*

Bryson, John, and Barbara Crosby. *Leadership for the Common Good: Tackling Public Problems in a Shared-Power World*. San Francisco, Calif.: Jossey-Bass, 1992. 415-433-1740.

Includes practical information, negotiation techniques, and networking strategies useful for overcoming problems associated with multiple-agency projects.

Carver, John. *Boards That Make a Difference: A New Design for Leadership in Nonprofit and Public Organizations.* San Francisco, Calif.: Jossey-Bass, 1990. 415-433-1740.

Examines board governance, board literature, and board practices. Analyzes common failures of board governance. Introduces the Policy Governance Model.

Carver, John, and Miriam Mayhew Carver. *Reinventing Your Board: A Step-by-Step Guide to Implementing Policy Governance.* San Francisco, Calif.: Jossey-Bass, 1997. 415-433-1740.

Provides guidelines for implementing the Policy Governance Model. Describes effective board decision making and crafting useful policies.

Casse, Pierre, and Surinder Deol. *Managing Intercultural Negotiations: Guidelines for Trainers and Negotiators.* Washington, D.C.: SIETAR International, 1985.

Cockman, Peter, Peter Reynolds, and Bill Evans. *Client-Centered Consulting: Getting Your Expertise Used When You're Not in Charge.* New York, N.Y.: McGraw Hill, 1996.

Describes beginning a consulting business. Includes sections on intervention skills, collecting data, problem diagnosis, and the implementation, disengagement, follow-up, and evaluation of a consulting assignment.

Connor, Richard A., Jr., and Jeffrey P. Davidson. *Marketing Your Consulting and Professional Services.* New York, N.Y.: John Wiley and Sons, 1985. 212-850-6418.

Covers marketing, promotion, and advertising for consultants. Concentrates on a client-centered view of marketing.

Dodd, Carley H. *Dynamics of Intercultural Communication.* Dubuque, Iowa: Brown and Benchmark, 1995.

Defines intercultural communication. Includes sections on: cultural and social diversity, understanding intercultural information, and applying intercultural competencies.

Drafke, Michael W., and Stan Kossen. *The Human Side of Organizations.* Reading, Mass.: Addison-Wesley, 1997.

Describes human relations in practical terms. Discusses problems of morale, supervision, leadership, and the importance of listening, the effects of change, and coping with frustration.

Drucker, Peter F. *Managing the Nonprofit Organization*. New York, N.Y.: HarperCollins, 1990.

Describes the tasks, responsibilities, and practices involved in effective management of nonprofit organizations. Contents include: analyzing the mission and performance of the organization, developing professional relationships, and practicing self-development.

Fuchs, Jerome H. *Making the Most of Management Consulting Services*. New York, N.Y.: AMACOM, 1975.

Describes the benefits of properly using a consulting service. Explains how management consultants make, save, and protect client profits.

Galbraith, Jay R., and Edward E. Lawler, III. *Organizing for the Future: The New Logic for Managing Complex Organizations*. San Francisco, Calif.: Jossey-Bass, 1993. 415-433-1740.

Explores key issues of organizational design. Identifies approaches for managing complex organizations in a changing global marketplace.

Gallessich, J. *The Profession and Practice of Consultation*. San Francisco, Calif.: Jossey-Bass, 1982. 415-433-1740.

📖 *Includes common processes, principles, and practices for beginning a consulting career.*

Galpin, Timothy J. *The Human Side of Change: A Practical Guide to Organization Redesign*. San Francisco, Calif.: Jossey-Bass, 1996. 415-433-1740.

Describes change as an ongoing process. Provides a step-by-step guide for implementing change.

Goodstein, L. *Consulting with Human Service Systems*. Reading, Mass.: Addison-Wesley, 1978.

📖 *Provides basic information on the consultative process in nonprofit and public organizations. Discusses organizational consultation, diagnosis, and intervention.*

Gray, Douglas A. *Start and Run a Profitable Consulting Business: A Step-by-Step Business Plan*. Bellingham, Wash.: Self-Counsel Press, 1989.

Includes sections on regulations and laws, selecting professional advisers, preparing a business plan, legally minimizing payment of taxes, avoiding liability, and preventing losses.

Greenbaum, Thomas L. *The Consultant's Manual: A Complete Guide to Building a Successful Consulting Practice.* New York, N.Y.: John Wiley and Sons, 1990. 212-850-6418.

Explains practical aspects of starting, building, and marketing a consulting business. Describes the research, planning, and problem-solving stages of a business plan.

Greiner, Larry E., and Robert O. Metzger. *Consulting to Management: Insights to Building and Managing a Successful Practice.* Englewood Cliffs, N.J.: Prentice-Hall, 1983.

Explains how to start and manage a consulting practice. Consists of five sections: the consulting profession, marketing consulting services, models and methods for consulting, stages in consulting, and reflections on consulting.

Gudykunst, William B., and Young Yun Kim. *Communicating with Strangers: An Approach to Intercultural Communication.* Reading, Mass.: Addison-Wesley, 1984.

Henning, Joel P. *The Future of Staff Groups: Daring to Distribute Power and Capacity.* San Francisco, Calif.: Barrett-Koehler, 1997. 800-929-2929.

Includes information on building staff group capacity, defining staff group accountability and service, repositioning staff groups, and reinventing staff group roles.

Hodgkinson, Virginia A., and Richard W. Lyman. *The Future of the Nonprofit Sector.* Washington, D.C.: Independent Sector, 1989. 202-223-8100.

Explores how complex changes today affect the future of nonprofit organizations. Offers strategies for coping with economic, social, and political trends.

Holtz, Herman. *The Business Plan Guide for Independent Consultants.* New York, N.Y.: John Wiley and Sons, 1994. 212-850-6418.

Provides information on writing a business plan. Includes worksheets and samples.

———. *Choosing and Using A Consultant: A Manager's Guide to Consulting Services.* New York, N.Y.: John Wiley and Sons, 1989. 212-850-6418.

Explains how to determine the need for a consultant, the type of consultant, and the resources for finding a consultant. Provides advice on soliciting and evaluating bids and proposals.

———. *The Complete Guide to Consulting Contracts*. Chicago, Ill.: Enterprise-Dearborn, 1997.

Describes the negotiation and drafting of effective contracts. Includes forty model agreements and clauses.

———. *The Consultant's Guide to Proposal Writing: How to Satisfy Your Clients and Double Your Income*. New York, N.Y.: John Wiley and Sons, 1990. 212-850-6418.

Describes selling your consulting skills to the government, avoiding common errors, bidding, safeguarding proposals from piracy, what clients look for in a proposal, copyrighting proposals, competitor strategies, and keys to creativity.

Hummel, Joan M. *Starting and Running a Nonprofit Organization*. Minneapolis, Minn.: University of Minnesota Press, 1996.

A basic primer on starting and running a nonprofit. Covers board of directors, bylaws, gaining 501(c)(3) status, creating a mission, budgeting, and more.

Johnson, Sandra J., and Mary Ann Smith. *Valuing Differences in the Workplace: Theory-to-Practice Monograph Series*. Alexandria, Va.: American Society for Training and Development, 1991. 703-683-8100.

Describes concepts involving effectively managing diversity and valuing differences in the workplace. Assists in the process of shifting to a multicultural focus in the organization.

Keltner, J.R. "Facilitation: Catalyst for Group Problem Solving." *Communication Quarterly* 3 (1) 8-32. 1989.

Kibbe, Barbara, and Fred Setterberg. *Succeeding with Consultants: Self-Assessment for the Changing Nonprofit*. Los Altos, Calif.: The David and Lucile Packard Foundation, 1992.

Identifies six areas in which consultants can benefit nonprofit organizations: governance, planning, fund development, financial management, quality assurance, and public relations.

Kiser, A. Glenn. *Masterful Facilitation: Becoming a Catalyst for Meaningful Change*. New York, N.Y.: AMACOM, 1998.

Teaches facilitators how to help organizations reach their goals. Explains techniques in articulating purpose, determining desired results, and choosing appropriate levels of intervention.

Kishel, Gregory, and Patricia Kishel. *How to Start and Run a Successful Consulting Business*. New York, N.Y.: John Wiley and Sons, 1996. 212-850-6418.

Includes sections on setting up businesses, determining fees, preparing proposals, satisfying clients, handling ethical matters, and generating additional income.

Knauft, E. B., Renee A. Berger, and Sandra T. Gray. *Profiles of Excellence: Achieving Success in the Nonprofit Sector*. Washington, D.C.: Independent Sector, 1991. 202-223-8100.

Identifies four principles of outstanding nonprofit leadership: primacy of mission, effective leadership, maintaining a dynamic board, and strong development programs.

Kochman, Thomas. *Black and White Styles in Conflict*. Chicago, Ill.: University of Chicago Press, 1981.

Analyzes differences in business styles, clarifies cultural reasons for communication differences, and provides a guide for crossing racial barriers.

Kretzmann, John, and John McKnight. *Building Communities from the Inside Out: A Path Toward Finding and Mobilizing a Community's Assets*. Chicago, Ill.: ACTA Publications, 1993.

A guide to mapping community assets and using those to improve community functioning.

Kubr, Milan. *Management Consulting: A Guide to the Profession*. Geneva, Switzerland: International Labour Office, 1986.

Includes sections on management consulting in perspective, the consulting process, consulting in various areas of management, managing a consulting organization, and developing management consults.

Lippitt, Gordon, and Ronald Lippitt. *The Consulting Process in Action*. San Francisco, Calif.: Jossey-Bass, 1986. 415-433-1740.

📖 *Emphasizes the consulting process phases, intervention decisions, consultant roles, ethical dilemmas, designing participative learning, diagnosis, evaluation, and international consulting.*

Loden, Marilyn, and Judy B. Rosener. *Workforce America: Managing Employee Diversity as a Vital Resource*. Homewood, Ill.: Business One Irwin, 1991.

Shows how to recognize organizational problems, foster teamwork, create comfortable working environments, develop leadership skills, and manage employee differences as assets.

Lohmann, Roger A. *The Commons: New Perspectives on Nonprofit Organizations and Voluntary Action.* San Francisco, Calif.: Jossey-Bass, 1992. 415-433-1740.

Describes the social, economic, and political structures and processes that characterize nonprofit organizations and encourage voluntary action.

Mattessich, Paul W., and Barbara R. Monsey. *Collaboration: What Makes It Work.* St. Paul, Minn.: Amherst H. Wilder Foundation, 1992.

In-depth analysis of the literature on collaborations. Extracts key factors that result in successful collaboration and suggests practical ways to apply those to collaborative projects.

———. *Community Building: What Makes It Work.* St. Paul, Minn.: Amherst H. Wilder Foundation, 1997.

An in-depth analysis of the literature on community building. Extracts key factors that result in successful community-building projects.

McKnight, John. *The Careless Society: Community and Its Counterfeits.* New York, N.Y.: Basic Books, 1995.

Analyzes why communities are rendered impotent by strong service systems. Describes the nature and growth of authentic citizen communities of care.

McLagan, Patricia A. *Models for Excellence: The Conclusions and Recommendations of the ASTD Training and Development Competence Guide.* Washington, D.C.: American Society for Training and Development, 1983.

Provides conclusions, models, and recommendations to help training and development managers and practitioners. Includes methodology and projects.

Nevis, Edwin C. *Organizational Consulting: A Gestalt Approach.* Hillsdale, N.J.: Analytic Press, 1987. 201-358-9477.

Presents organizational effectiveness from psychological aspects. Applies Gestalt model to organizations and interventions in organizational settings.

O'Connell, Brian. *The Board Member's Book: Making a Difference in Voluntary Organizations.* New York, N.Y.: The Foundation Center, 1993. 800-424-9836.

Discusses finding, developing, and rewarding good board members. Helps board members make the most of volunteering.

O'Neill, Patrick, and Edison J. Trickett. *Community Consultation*. San Francisco, Calif.: Jossey-Bass, 1992. 415-433-1740.

 📖 *Describes consultation within the community, including setting, community groups, clients, resources, and context.*

Parsons, Richard Dean, and Joel Meyers. *Developing Consulting Skills*. San Francisco, Calif.: Jossey-Bass, 1984. 415-433-1740.

 Describes methods used by human services professionals for training, development, and assessment.

Pfeffer, Jeffrey. *Managing with Power: Politics and Influence in Organizations*. Boston, Mass.: Harvard Business School Press, 1992.

 Details the role of power and influence in organizations. Includes sections on sources of power, strategies for employing power, and power dynamics.

Pfeiffer, William J., ed. *The 1996 Annual: Consulting Vol. 1*. San Diego, Calif.: Pfeiffer, 1996. 800-274-4434.

 One of a series of annual publications on consulting and training. Available from Pfeiffer, now an imprint of Jossey-Bass.

Reddy, W. Brendan. *Intervention Skills: Process Consultation for Small Groups and Teams*. San Diego, Calif.: Pfeiffer, 1995. 800-274-4434.

 Focuses on putting the concept of group-process consultation into practice. Describes how to help groups identify, diagnose, and resolve occurring problems.

Robinson, Dana Gaines, and James C. Robinson. *Training for Impact: How to Link Training to Business Needs and Measure the Results*. San Francisco, Calif.: Jossey-Bass, 1989. 415-433-1740.

 Describes benefits obtained from training programs, such as implementing results-oriented training, transferring training program skills to jobs, and evaluating training results.

Rothwell, William J., Roland Sullivan, and Gary N. McLean. *Practicing Organization Development*. San Francisco, Calif.: Jossey-Bass, 1995. 415-433-1740.

 Defines action research. Relates action research to organizational development. Describes organizational development interventions.

Salamon, Lester M. *Holding the Center: America's Nonprofit Sector at a Crossroads*. New York, N.Y.: Nathan Cummings Foundation, 1997.

 Examines the changing role of nonprofits within fields such as health care, education, social services, and international aid. Pro-

vides charts and tables to illustrate spending, growth, and other trends within these fields.

Salmon, Bill, and Nate Rosenblatt. *The Complete Book of Consulting.* Ridgefield, Conn.: Round Lake Publishing, 1995. 203-438-5255.

Discusses strategies for becoming a successful consultant. Contains 150 forms useful in starting and running a consulting business.

Schaffer, Robert H. *High-Impact Consulting: How Clients and Consultants Can Leverage Rapid Results into Long-Term Gains.* San Francisco, Calif.: Jossey-Bass, 1997. 415-433-1740.

📕 *Explains the basics in creating a powerful partnership between consultant and client. Identifies the five fatal flaws of conventional consulting. Describes a method for designing consulting projects that produce results.*

Schein, Edgar H. *Process Consultation: Its Role in Organizational Development.* Reading, Mass.: Addison-Wesley, 1969.

Introduces and discusses the concept of process consultation. Helps managers become good diagnosticians. Explains intervention procedures.

Schiffman, Stephan. *The Consultant's Handbook: How to Start and Develop Your Own Practice.* Holbrook, Mass.: Bob Adams, Inc., 1988. 800-872-5627.

Discusses how to predict and prepare for common business problems, attract clients, determine rates, and write proposals. Includes sample proposals.

Schwarz, Roger M. *The Skilled Facilitator: Practical Wisdom for Developing Effective Groups.* San Francisco, Calif.: Jossey-Bass, 1994. 415-433-1740.

Describes how expertly managed groups can improve an organization's effectiveness, increase employee commitment, and improve company flexibility. Integrates the theory and practice of group facilitation.

Seltzer, Michael. *Securing Your Organization's Future: A Complete Guide to Fund-Raising Strategies.* New York, N.Y.: The Foundation Center, 1987. 800-424-9836.

Describes strategies for acquiring long-term financial well-being. Explains fund-raising strategies.

Senge, Peter M. *The Fifth Discipline: The Art and Practice of the Learning Organization*. New York, N.Y.: Doubleday, 1990.

Describes five disciplines considered important in building a learning organization.

Shenson, Howard L. *How to Select and Manage Consultants: A Guide to Getting What You Pay For*. Lexington, Mass.: Lexington Books, 1990.

Explains how to select and manage consultants. Includes the identification, evaluation, selection, and management of consultants.

Steckel, Richard, Robin Simons, and Peter Lengsfelder. *Filthy Rich and Other Nonprofit Fantasies: Changing the Way Nonprofits Do Business in the 90's*. Berkeley, Calif.: Ten Speed Press, 1989.

Describes how nonprofits can earn revenue. Demonstrates operating a business venture in the charitable sector.

Stern, Gary J. *Marketing Workbook for Nonprofit Organizations*. St. Paul, Minn.: Amherst H. Wilder Foundation, 1990.

Explains nonprofit marketing and how to write a marketing plan. Includes worksheets to guide the process.

————. *Marketing Workbook for Nonprofit Organizations, Vol. II: Mobilize People for Marketing Success*. St. Paul, Minn.: Amherst H. Wilder Foundation, 1997.

Describes how to mobilize an entire organization, its staff, volunteers, and supporters, to accomplish a marketing goal using a one-to-one marketing campaign. Includes worksheets to guide the process.

Tannen, Deborah. *That's Not What I Meant! How Conversational Style Makes or Breaks Relationships*. New York, N.Y.: Ballantine, 1986.

Describes the nature of conversation and interpersonal communication and their impact on relationships.

Tepper, Ron. *Become a Top Consultant: How the Experts Do It*. New York, N.Y.: John Wiley and Sons, 1987. 212-850-6418.

Includes samples of contracts, proposals, letters, diagrams, and case studies relating to consulting. Describes how issues regarding consultants are handled.

Thomas, Roosevelt R., Jr. *Beyond Race and Gender: Unleashing the Power of Your Total Work Force by Managing Diversity*. New York, N.Y.: AMACOM, 1991.

Describes the process of creating and managing cultural diversity.

Trompenaars, Alfons. *Riding the Waves of Culture: Understanding Cultural Diversity in Business.* London: The Economist Books, 1993.

Weisbord, Marvin R. *Organizational Diagnosis. A Workbook of Theory and Practice.* Reading, Mass.: Addison-Wesley, 1978.

Teaches the reader important elements about evaluating organizations. Includes a model with categories on structure, purposes, relationships, rewards, helpful mechanisms, and leadership.

————. *Productive Workplaces: Organizing and Managing for Dignity, Meaning, and Community.* San Francisco, Calif.: Jossey-Bass, 1987. 415-433-1740.

Describes searching for productive workplaces, rethinking organizational improvement, and managing and consulting beyond design limits.

Wheatley, Margaret. *Leadership and the New Science: Learning about Organizations from an Orderly Universe.* San Francisco, Calif.: Barrett-Koehler, 1994. 800-929-2929.

Summarizes new science discoveries and discusses the search for a simpler way to lead organizations. Provides insights for organizing work, people, and life.

Winer, Michael, and Karen Ray. *Collaboration Handbook: Creating, Sustaining, and Enjoying the Journey.* St. Paul, Minn.: Amherst H. Wilder Foundation, 1994.

Describes a process for starting and operating a collaborative. Includes worksheets to assist the process.

Withers, Jean, and Carol Vipperman. *Marketing Your Service: A Planning Guide for Small Business.* North Vancouver, Brit. Col.: International Self-Counsel Press, 1987.

Explains basic marketing. Provides thirty-two worksheets to assist in developing a specific marketing plan.

Young, Dennis R., Robert M. Hollister, Virginia A. Hodgkinson, and Associates. *Governing, Leading, and Managing Nonprofit Organizations: New Insights from Research and Practice.* Washington, D.C.: Independent Sector, 1993. 202-223-8100.

Provides insights in meeting the challenges of governance and management. Describes nonprofit management practices.

Journals/Periodicals

Chronicle of Philanthropy: The Newspaper of the Nonprofit World. Washington, D.C.: The Chronicle of Higher Education, Inc. 202-466-1207.

> *A biweekly newspaper covering issues related to managing nonprofit groups, technology, gifts and giving, grant makers, special interests of donors and board members, and fund-raising.*

Foundation News. Washington, D.C.: Council on Foundations, Inc. 202-466-6512.

> *Bimonthly publication that covers topics related to foundations and philanthropic trends.*

Nonprofit Management and Leadership Journal. San Francisco, Calif.: Jossey-Bass. (800) 956-7739. www.jbp.com

> *A quarterly journal offering readers the authoritative insights of top executives and scholars on the common concerns of nonprofit leaders in all settings.*

Nonprofit World: The National Nonprofit Leadership and Management Journal. Madison, Wisc.: Society for Nonprofit Organizations. 800-424-7367.

> *A magazine that includes in-depth articles on nonprofit management and leadership and sections on global thinking, fund-raising, the boardroom, legal counsel, resources, nonprofit providers, people and technology, relevant reviews, and nonprofit briefs.*

PULSE! Online Newsletter of the Nonprofit Management Support Community. San Francisco, Calif.: Support Centers of America. www.supportcenter.org/sca.

> *A free on-line (e-mail) newsletter covering developments in the nonprofit sector.*

Publishers and Organizations That Can Provide Resources

Amherst H. Wilder Foundation
Publishing Center
919 Lafond Avenue
Saint Paul, MN 55104
800-274-6024
www.wilder.org

Applied Research and Development Institute (ARDI)
2121 South Oneida Street, Suite 633
Denver, CO 80224-2555
303-691-6076
E-mail: ardiintl@aol.com
www.ardi.org

The Foundation Center
79 Fifth Avenue, Eighth Floor
New York, NY 10003-3076
212-620-4230
http://fdncenter.org

Handsnet
E-mail: hninfo@handsnet.org
www.handsnet.org

Independent Sector
1828 L Street, NW, Twelfth Floor
Washington, DC 20036
202-223-8100

Jossey-Bass Publishers
350 Sansome Street
San Francisco, CA 94104
800-956-7739
www.josseybass.com

National Center for Nonprofit Boards
2000 L Street, NW, Suite 510
Washington, DC 20036-4907
202-452-6262, 800-883-6262
www.ncnb.org

National Council of Nonprofit Associations
1001 Connecticut Avenue, NW, Suite 900
Washington, DC 20036
202-833-5740
www.ncna.org

National Training Laboratories (NTL)
300 North Lee Street, Suite 300
Alexandria, VA 22314-2607
800-777-5227
www.ntl.org

Membership Associations

American Society for Training and Development
(National membership organization for consultants and trainers; chapters in many states)
1640 King Street, Box 1443
Alexandria, VA 22313-2043
703-683-8100
www.astd.org

National Association of Grantwriters and Nonprofit Consultants
(Membership organization for nonprofit consultants)
P.O. Box 167365
Irving, TX 75016
www.naogwanc.com

National Alliance for Nonprofit Management *(formerly Nonprofit Management Association and Support Centers of America; the organizations merged in 1998)*
(Membership organization for consultants and management support organizations)
1899 L Street, NW, 3rd Floor
Washington, DC 20036
202-955-8406
www.allianceonline.org

National Society of Fund Raising Executives
1101 King Street, Suite 700
Alexandria, VA 22314
703-684-0410
www.nsfre.org

Sample Consulting Proposals

Formal Approach

PROPOSAL TO: North Village Development

Introduction

North Village Development (NVD) is a community partnership working to rebuild the economic, social, and physical prosperity of the North Village community. Over the last two years, NVD has defined objectives for their work and established a broad community-based network of over one hundred individuals and over sixty neighborhood, business, and public agencies working in support of North Village redevelopment. NVD has determined that they now need to strengthen their efforts through development of a strategic plan, addressing such questions as structure, staffing, business development and retention, and sustainability.

NVD has requested assistance in developing a strategic plan for the next three years, using a planning approach that would involve the many interested people and groups in the community and use time efficiently. The following proposal includes objectives, a work plan, and budget for this project.

Project objective

Develop a three-year strategic plan for NVD that describes the project's:

- Mission
- Objectives
- Strategies to accomplish the objectives
- Structure and staffing: task force and member roles and responsibilities, staffing levels and roles, leadership succession, bylaws of the initiative
- Finances and resource development
- Three-year steps/timeline to implement the plan

Planning approach

The recommended planning approach involves a planning committee throughout the planning process and solicits community, business, and government input at two stages of the planning through focus groups. It also surveys many of the individuals involved in the effort to date, resulting in community buy-in and a comprehensive plan within a short period of time.

Work plan

Steps	Responsible	By When
1. Get agreement on project objectives, work plan, and budget.	NVD Steering Committee, Staff, Consultant	Jan. 1
2. Orient consultants to NVD's history and accomplishments, structure, and finances.	Staff, Consultant	Jan. 15
3. In first meeting of the planning committee: • Finalize planning process • Decide data collection scope/audience, methods, questions, cover letter	Planning Committee, Staff, Consultant	Feb. 1
4. Collect data as planned, including (budget assumptions): • Survey of fifty individuals • Up to three focus groups with key stakeholders (e.g., business, community leaders, government) • Follow-up phone interviews with selected survey nonrespondents	Consultant	Apr. 1

Steps	Responsible	By When
5. Summarize information collected.	Consultant	Apr. 15
6. In second meeting of the planning committee: • Review data • Identify critical issues/key strategy areas • Plan task force strategy development effort (assignment, worksheets, leadership, membership, timeline, support needed)	Planning Committee, Staff, Consultant	May 1
7. Develop strategies/recommendations in areas as decided. Budget assumes five hours consultant support for three task forces.	Task Forces, Staff, Consultant	Jul. 1
8. Compile task force work into first draft of plan.	Consultant, Staff	Aug. 1
9. Draft financing plans. Incorporate into first draft of plan.	Staff, Consultant	Aug. 15
10. In third meeting of the planning committee: • Review first draft plan • Decide revisions/contingency plans needed • Decide review process	Planning Team, Staff, Consultant	Sept. 1
11. Review draft plan with three focus groups: business, community, and government. Possibly include funders in review process. Incorporate suggested changes as appropriate.	Staff, Consultant	Nov. 1
12. In fourth meeting of the planning committee, finalize strategic plan utilizing community/business/ government input.	Planning Team, Staff, Consultant	Nov. 15
13. Approve plan.	Steering Committee	Dec. 1
14. Implement plan: • Monitor and modify as appropriate (every six months) • Update plan annually	North Village Development	ongoing

Products

The consultant is responsible for:

- Agendas and summaries for meetings and focus groups
- Survey and focus group design and summaries
- Producing a first-draft plan

NVD is responsible for:

- Scheduling meetings
- Meeting costs: room, equipment, refreshments
- Copying and distributing all materials prior to and following meetings and focus groups, including surveys
- Producing the final plan

Consultant(s)

The consulting team will be led by _____. Others working on the project include _____ and _____.
See attached résumés

Costs

- Consultant: up to 75 hours @ $75/hour = $5,625
- Project support: up to 24 hours @ $25/hour = $600

TOTAL $6,225

If it is anticipated because of additional work, canceled meetings, or other reasons that costs will exceed the estimates, the consultant will discuss options with NVD as soon as possible.

Billing

The consultant will submit monthly invoices to NVD, which outline time and charges to date. Unless other arrangements are made in advance, invoices are payable within thirty (30) days. Either the consultant or NVD may terminate this project with ten (10) days' written notice.

Authorization to proceed

Name _____   Date _____
Board Chair, North Village Development

Name _____   Date _____
Executive Director, North Village Development

Name _____   Date _____
Consultant

Informal Approach—Letter of Agreement

Lavinia Torwak
Community Health Clinic
4333 Zelton Street
Anywhere, USA

Dear Lavinia,

Thank you for asking me to assist Community Health Clinic with a community health needs assessment. This letter is to confirm my understanding of our agreement for that project.

You have two objectives: (1) to conduct a community health needs assessment through five focus groups; and (2) to update your strategic plan based on the findings from the needs assessment. We agreed that you are not clear at this stage what process you want to use for the second objective, so we will not estimate costs for that work at this time. My cost for the first objective is 36 hours @ $75/hour for a total of $2,700. I will bill you for actual time up to a maximum of $2,700. If the scope of work changes, we will need to discuss possible changes in cost.

Our first meeting of the steering committee for the needs assessment is scheduled for September 28 from 1:00 to 3:00. Prior to that meeting I will draft an agenda and an outline of the decisions we need to make to get the needs assessment moving, and run those by you. The only other scheduling we discussed was to try to extend invitations to the focus groups by October 12. Focus groups can be scheduled anytime after October 26.

It will be a pleasure to work with you, Lavinia. Please let me know if you have any questions or concerns.

Regards,

Consultant

APPENDIX C

Client Worksheets

This worksheet can be used with a planning committee for brainstorming and discussion, or as a format guide for writing a plan.

Goal 1

Possible strategies to accomplish this goal:

1.

2.

3.

Goal 2

Possible strategies to accomplish this goal:

1.

2.

3.

Goal 3

Possible strategies to accomplish this goal:

1.

2.

3.

Goal 4

Possible strategies to accomplish this goal:

1.

2.

3.

This worksheet can help an organization or group decide between alternative strategies to reach a goal.

State the goal the group wants to accomplish:

Using the chart on the next page:

1. In column one list the alternative strategies that the group is considering.

2. List criteria that selected strategies need to meet (e.g., fit with mission and values, filling a gap in the community, or financial feasibility):

   A.

   B.

   C.

   D.

   E.

3. For each strategy listed, rate the extent to which it meets each of the criteria using a 1–5 scale, where 1 = little fit, and 5 = great fit.

4. Add up the ratings for each strategy on all criteria. In the last column put the total rating score for each strategy.

5. Select strategies that are most consistent with the criteria (i.e., the strategies with the highest rating).

Strategies	Criteria					Overall Strategy Rating
	A	B	C	D	E	
1.						
2.						
3.						
4.						
5.						
6.						

Task Force: _____

Each task force should complete the following worksheet, thinking of what it expects
or hopes to accomplish over the next _____ years. Turn in the completed worksheet
to _____ by _____ .

1. **Goals/Objectives for the year** ____: *What do you hope to accomplish by the year* ____*?*	2. **Strategies:** *What strategies and steps will you pursue to accomplish each objective?*	3. **Timeline:** *By when do you hope to accomplish each strategy / step?*
A.	a. b. c.	
B.	a. b. c.	
C.	a. b. c.	
D.	a. b. c.	
E.	a. b. c.	

4. **Funding:**

What funding sources or methods need to be pursued to support these strategies?

5. **Communications:**

What communications efforts are needed to support these strategies?

6. **Alliances:**

What new partnerships or alliances will be needed to accomplish your objectives?

This worksheet can be used as an implementation plan for a planning or change effort. If desired, the steps can be divided into sections by goal or objective.

Steps	Lead Person	By When
1.		
2.		
3.		
4.		
5.		
6.		
7.		
8.		
9.		
10.		
11.		
12.		
13.		
14.		
15.		

APPENDIX D

Consultant Worksheets

Use this worksheet to assess your capabilities and development needs as a consultant.

General Consulting Practice	Don't Know This	Area of Strength	Want to Learn More
Ability to manage projects and budgets			
Strong writing and speaking skills appropriate to a professional environment			
Contracting skills			
Personal time management			
Understanding of nonprofit and community organizations			
Awareness of and ease in dealing with cultural, race, sex, age, and class differences			
Knowledge of the major cultural groups, their values and cultural norms			
Knowledge of the stages of development of individuals, groups, organizations, and communities			
Skill in using a variety of data collection methods			
Basic technological literacy and competence			
Marketing and promotions for your practice			
Business planning and management			
Electronic communications: fax, e-mail, fax broadcasting, teleconferencing			
Personal Development			
Capacity for reflection and self-assessment			
Securing and utilizing feedback regarding one's effectiveness			
Clarifying and articulating the values and beliefs that guide one's work			
Designing and implementing a personal growth plan			
Developing and using a support system for self			

[17] Some of these competencies have been adapted from the certification policies of Certified Consultants International. The author was active in the organization, which ended operations in 1986, and helped develop some of the original certification competencies.

	Don't Know This	Area of Strength	Want to Learn More
Working at the Interpersonal Level			
Competence in basic interpersonal communications skills, including paraphrasing and summarizing, giving and receiving feedback, and resolving conflicts			
Ability to design and utilize interviewing as a data gathering tool			
Understanding of and ability to use coaching as a developmental process			
Working at the Group Level			
Capacity to establish a safe, learning-oriented environment in a group			
Ability to facilitate and influence groups so that tasks, relationships, and individual needs are addressed			
Understanding of and ability to facilitate intergroup dynamics			
Understanding of and ability to use mediation and negotiation skills			
Advanced Group Level Competencies			
Understanding of, and ability to apply, stages of group development			
Ability to deal with issues of inclusion, control, intimacy, and power in a group setting			
Capacity to assist a group to learn about and process group dynamics			
Ability to facilitate learning about task and maintenance functions in a group: goal setting, planning, decision making, participation, conflict			

	Don't Know This	Area of Strength	Want to Learn More
Working at the Organization Level			
Knowledge and skill in scanning an organization's environment and assisting the organization in responding to it			
Knowledge of and ability to assess the functions of an organization and how they interrelate			
Understanding of organizational systems and the interrelationship between parts of systems			
Ability to facilitate a basic planning process including goal setting, strategy formation, and action planning			
Advanced Organization Level Competencies			
Capacity to apply a variety of theoretical models of organization behavior and performance			
Skills in intervening in a variety of organizational functions			
Working at the Community or Large Systems Level			
Experience with a broad range of types of organizations from all sectors: for-profit, nonprofit, government, and grassroots			
Understanding of the process and dynamics of collaboration and the ability to facilitate collaboration			
Ability to design and utilize intergroup and interorganizational processes			
Capability to assume advocacy, power building, and negotiating as well as facilitating roles			
Understanding of basic community organizing methods			
Training and Development			
Understanding of adult learning principles			
Ability to design learning experiences to meet individual differences in learning and organizational requirements			
Competency in identifying the knowledge and skill requirements of jobs, tasks, and roles			
Ability to observe and describe behaviors and their effects			

This version focuses on the client's perception of quality and satisfaction with the consultation and the extent to which you performed commonly valued consulting behaviors.

Thank you for agreeing to provide me with feedback on my consulting services.

1. Please briefly describe the original concern or request that led you to ask for assistance:

2. In considering the overall quality of service you received, would you say it was (please circle one):

Terrible	Poor	Okay	Good	Very Good	Outstanding

3. Please tell me if I:

Please tell me if I:	Strongly Disagree	Disagree	Neutral	Agree	Strongly Agree
Effectively addressed your request					
Met deadlines					
Genuinely seemed to care about you and your organization					
Seemed knowledgeable about my work					
Helped you develop your capacity as an organization					
Used time well					
Made a useful contribution					

4. How satisfied were you overall with the services you received (please circle one)?

Very Dissatisfied	Dissatisfied	Satisfied	Very Satisfied

Is there anything I could have done differently that would have improved the service you received? ☐ Yes ☐ No   If yes, please describe:

Thank you for your feedback. Please contact me if you have any questions or concerns. It has been a pleasure to work with you.

---

[18] Adapted from evaluation design created by Wilder Research Center, a division of Amherst H. Wilder Foundation.

This version asks for the client's assessment of the extent to which the consulting objectives were met and asks for feedback on consulting quality in a different way from the first version.

Thank you for agreeing to provide me with feedback on my consulting services.

1. According to our project proposal/agreement, the following were the objectives of our work with you on the recent consulting project. To what extent were each of the objectives met? (list objectives below)

Objective	Not Met	Partially Met	Met	Exceeded	Don't Know
A.					
B.					
C.					
D.					
E.					

For those objectives that were not met or partially met, could I have done anything differently so that the objectives were met?

2. The following questions relate to the quality of my services:

	Terrible	Poor	Acceptable	Good	Excellent	Don't Know
How would you rate my ability to listen to and understand the needs of your group?						
How would you rate my ability to communicate in a clear and understandable fashion?						
How would you rate my ability to work with you in developing a plan and objectives for your group?						
How would you rate the overall quality of service you received?						

Add additional items related to your consultation here

---

[19] Adapted from evaluation design created by Wilder Research Center, a division of Amherst H. Wilder Foundation.

3. To what extent has your organization's capacity to address similar issues in the future been enhanced (please circle one)?

Not at all	Somewhat	Greatly

4. What did you find *most* helpful about my consultation services?

5. If you could change one thing about the services you received, what would it be?

Thank you for your feedback. Please contact me if you have any questions or concerns. It has been a pleasure to work with you.

Part 1: Create a vision for your practice.

Write your vision for what you want your consulting practice to look like in 3 5 years. Use the trigger questions on page 139 to help think through aspects of your vision.

Part 2: Assess the feasibility of achieving that vision.

Answer the following questions to assess the size of the potential market for the kind of work you hope to do.

1. Who are your potential clients?

List categories of potential clients (e.g., hospitals, public schools, youth organizations, theaters)	Name some of the organizations in each category	How many organizations are in your geographic area (local, regional, national) within each category?

2. What are the challenges, needs, and wants of your potential clients (from the list in question 1)? Do these fit with the kind of work you want to do? How can you find out what they need and want?

What are the issues and challenges facing your potential clients?	*What do you need to learn more about?*

3. Who else is doing this work? Are they potential allies or partners? Is the market saturated with consultants doing this work? Or are there few other resources in this field?

List other consultants who do the same work you hope to do.	*Note potential allies, partners, or sources of information.*

4. Do you have the skills, expertise, and credentials to do this work?

A. List the skills, expertise, and credentials that are required to do this kind of work.

B. Describe what a potential client might expect a consultant to have in training, experience, and credentials.

C. Assess your development needs:

What training, experience, or credentials do you need to acquire to do this work well?	*How can you obtain these?*

5. Conclusions: What do you need to learn or do to align your vision with the realities of the market and your own capabilities? (Include follow-up steps from each of the previous questions)

Part 3: List your marketing goals.

Use the list of questions under marketing goals on page 141 to stimulate areas you might concentrate on. Also refer to conclusions reached in Part 2, question 5 of this worksheet.

1.

2.

3.

4.

Part 4: List strategies and action steps you will pursue to achieve your vision.

Use the suggestions on pages 142–43 under "Reputation-Building Strategies" and "Relation-ship-Building Strategies" for ideas and add your own. For each strategy, list action steps you will take and a timeline for accomplishing it.

Strategies I will pursue	Action steps	Timeline
A.		
B.		
C.		
D.		
E.		
F.		
G.		

Budget assumptions:

List the billing assumptions you will use to build your consulting project budget. Include assumptions such as rates for different kinds of work, use of time, travel, cost of other staff, and other billable expenses.

1.

2.

3.

Cost estimates:

Step (from proposal work plan)	Hours	Fee	Expenses	Total Cost
1.				
2.				
3.				
4.				
5.				
6.				
7.				
8.				
9.				
10.				
11.				
12.				
13.				
14.				
TOTALS				

The Difference between Employee and Independent Contractor

As a consultant, you must be careful that you do not inadvertently become, at least in the eyes of the Internal Revenue Service, an employee of the group with whom you are consulting. Following is a reprint of IRS publication 15A, available from the IRS.

Employee or Independent Contractor?[20]

An employer must generally withhold income taxes, withhold and pay Social Security and Medicare taxes, and pay unemployment taxes on wages paid to an employee. An employer does not generally have to withhold or pay any taxes on payments to independent contractors.

Common-law rules

To determine whether an individual is an employee or an independent contractor under the common law, the relationship of the worker and the business must be examined. All evidence of control and independence must be considered. In any employee-independent contractor determination, all information that provides evidence of the degree of control and the degree of independence must be considered.

Facts that provide evidence of the degree of control and independence fall into three categories: behavioral control, financial control, and the type of relationship of the parties as shown below.

---

[20] Internal Revenue Service, Publication 15A, downloaded from http//:www.irs.gov.

Behavioral control

Facts that show whether the business has a right to direct and control how the worker does the task for which the worker is hired include the type and degree of—

- Instructions the business gives the worker. An employee is generally subject to the business's instructions about when, where, and how to work. Even if no instructions are given, sufficient behavioral control may exist if the employer has the right to control how the work results are achieved.

- Training the business gives the worker. An employee may be trained to perform services in a particular manner. Independent contractors ordinarily use their own methods.

Financial control

Facts that show whether the business has a right to control the business aspects of the worker's job include:

- The extent to which the worker has unreimbursed business expenses. Independent contractors are more likely to have unreimbursed expenses than employees. Fixed ongoing costs that are incurred regardless of whether work is currently being performed are especially important. However, employees may also incur unreimbursed expenses in connection with the services they perform for their business.

- The extent of the worker's investment. An independent contractor often has a significant investment in the facilities he or she uses in performing services for someone else. However, a significant investment is not required.

- The extent to which the worker makes services available to the relevant market.

- How the business pays the worker. An employee is generally paid by the hour, week, or month. An independent contractor is usually paid by the job. However, it is common in some professions, such as law, to pay independent contractors hourly.

- The extent to which the worker can realize a profit or incur a loss. An independent contractor can make a profit or loss.

Type of relationship

Facts that show the parties' type of relationship include:

- Written contracts describing the relationship the parties intended to create.

- Whether the business provides the worker with employee-type benefits, such as insurance, a pension plan, vacation pay, or sick pay.

- The permanency of the relationship. If you engage a worker with the expectation that the relationship will continue indefinitely, rather than for a specific project or period, this is generally considered evidence that your intent was to create an employer-employee relationship.

- The extent to which services performed by the worker are a key aspect of the regular business of the company. If a worker provides services that are a key aspect of your regular business activity, it is more likely that you will have the right to direct and control his or her activities. For example, if a law firm hires an attorney, it is likely that it will present the attorney's work as its own and would have the right to control or direct that work. This would indicate an employer-employee relationship.

IRS Help

If you want the IRS to determine whether a worker is an employee, file Form SS-8, Determination of Employee Work Status for Purposes of Federal Employment Taxes and Income Tax Withholding, with the IRS.

The Nonprofit Management Association Professional Standards for Management Assistance Providers[21]

We intend to maintain a high level of ethics and professional service. In return for the faith that nonprofit organizations place in us, we accept the obligation to conduct our practice in a way that will be beneficial to the public good. These standards are put forth to give clients a basis for confidence that we will serve them in accordance with professional standards of competence, objectivity, and integrity. We adhere to the following professional standards:

1. We recognize that the professional delivery of management support services requires objectivity, independence, and integrity. We assume responsibility for seeing that clients benefit from services delivered and that fee revenue is not a measure of success.

2. We deliver only those services that we are qualified to undertake and which we believe are beneficial to the client and to those they serve. We assign only those personnel who are competent to give effective service in solving the particular problem and/or addressing the issues involved.

3. We ensure that the client understands the objectives and scope of services and the costs before they are delivered. This information is confirmed and subsequent significant changes are discussed with and agreed to by the client in writing. When it is difficult or impossible to give a reasonable estimate of the fee before any work is started, we will provide such an estimate as soon as feasible.

---

[21] Reprinted with permission of the Nonprofit Management Association, which as of this printing has merged with the Support Centers of America to become the National Alliance for Nonprofit Management. The new organization plans to revise these standards.

4. In our consulting work, we refrain from undertaking or continuing an assignment where it is clear that the client's only purpose is to use our name and reputation to lend weight to decisions already made or actions already planned, or where the consultant's freedom of independent analysis and recommendation is restricted. Further, we reserve the right to withdraw if conditions develop which interfere with the successful conduct of the assignment.

5. We carefully evaluate the quality of the work done by our personnel. These evaluations are used to continuously improve the quality of service.

6. Any fees charged are reasonable and appropriate to the character of the work and the responsibility assumed. We believe it is our responsibility to see that overall benefits accrue to clients as a result of these services.

7. We hold in confidence all information gathered during the course of our professional relationships.

8. We refrain from serving concurrently two or more clients who are deemed to be competitors in areas of vital interests without informing each client.

9. We disclose to our clients any relationships, circumstances, or interests that might influence our objectivity.

10. We accept our responsibility to the profession to share with colleagues the methods and techniques being used in serving clients. We will not, without their permission, use proprietary materials which others have developed.

11. In our consulting work, we refrain from undertaking work with a client where another consulting firm is currently serving the client unless we are assured, and can satisfy ourselves, that there is no reason to expect conflict between the two assignments.

12. We provide for ongoing staff and volunteer development to keep our personnel abreast of the latest thinking and advances in the field of nonprofit management.

13. We maintain open and honest communication with the client, keeping the client informed of any significant changes affecting service delivery.

Approved by Nonprofit Management Association, December, 1992.

Index

Collaboration Handbook:
Creating, Sustaining, and Enjoying the Journey

by Michael Winer and Karen Ray

Shows you how to get a collaboration going, define the results you're after, determine everyone's roles, create an action plan, and evaluate the results. Tells you what to expect and how to handle challenges. Includes a case study of one collaboration from start to finish, helpful tips on how to avoid pitfalls, and worksheets to keep everyone on track.

192 pages, softcover, $28.00

Collaboration: What Makes It Work

by Wilder Research Center

An in-depth review of current collaboration research. Major findings are summarized, critical conclusions are drawn, and nineteen key factors influencing successful collaborations are identified. See if your collaboration's plans include the necessary ingredients.

53 pages, softcover, $14.00

Community Building: What Makes It Work

by Wilder Research Center

Shows you what really does (and doesn't) contribute to community building success. Reveals twenty-eight keys to help you build community more effectively. Includes detailed descriptions of each factor, case examples of how they play out, and practical questions to assess your own work.

112 pages, softcover, $20.00

Coping with Cutbacks:
The Nonprofit Guide to Success When Times Are Tight

by Emil Angelica and Vincent Hyman

Describes the big changes coming as a result of devolution—the delegation of power from the federal government to local governments. Among these changes: far less government funding for nonprofits. This book helps you understand why and how devolution is occurring—and what you can do to prepare. It *doesn't* tell you to retrench or get "lean and mean." Today's situation is different, and the authors advocate a different set of solutions—

expanding and deepening your nonprofit's connection to the community; revisiting and, if necessary, revising your mission; and considering other approaches that get at the heart of mission work. Your organization doesn't have to be in a financial crisis in order to benefit from this book.

128 pages, softcover, $25.00

Marketing Workbook for Nonprofit Organizations Volume I

by Gary J. Stern

Don't just wish for results—get them! Here's how to create a straightforward, usable marketing plan. Includes the six P's of Marketing, how to use them effectively, a sample marketing plan, and detachable worksheets.

132 pages, softcover, $25.00

Marketing Workbook for Nonprofit Organizations Volume II:
Mobilize People for Marketing Success

by Gary J. Stern

Put together a successful promotional campaign based on the most persuasive tool of all: personal contact. Learn how to mobilize your entire organization, its staff, volunteers, and supporters in a focused, one-to-one marketing campaign. Provides step-by-step instructions, sample agendas for motivational trainings, and worksheets to keep the campaign organized and on track. Also includes *Pocket Guide for Marketing Representatives*. In it, your marketing representatives can record key campaign messages and find motivational reminders.

192 pages, softcover, $25.00

Strategic Planning Workbook for Nonprofit Organizations, Revised and Updated

by Bryan Barry

Chart a wise course for your nonprofit's future. This time-tested workbook gives you practical step-by-step guidance, real-life examples, one nonprofit's complete strategic plan, and easy-to-use worksheets.

144 pages, softcover, $25.00

The Wilder Publishing Center has also published the following books on violence prevention and intervention:

The Little Book of Peace

Designed & illustrated by Kelly O. Finnerty

A pocket-size guide to help people think about violence and talk about it with their families and friends. Over 250,000 copies of this booklet are in use in schools, homes, churches, businesses, and prisons. You may download a free copy of *The Little Book of Peace* from our Web site at www.wilder.org.

24 pages, $.65 each (minimum order 10 copies)

Foundations for Violence-Free Living
A Step-by-Step Guide to Facilitating Men's Domestic Abuse Groups

by David J. Mathews, MA, LICSW

A complete guide to facilitating a men's domestic abuse program. Includes twenty-nine activities, detailed guidelines for presenting each activity, and a discussion of psychological issues that may arise out of each activity. Also gives you tips for intake, individual counseling, facilitating groups, working with resistant clients, and recommended policies and releases.

240 pages, softcover, $45.00

On the Level
(Participant's Workbook to *Foundations for Violence-Free Living*)

Contains forty-nine worksheets including midterm and final evaluations. Men can record their insights and progress. A permanent binding makes the workbook easy to carry home for outside assignments, and you don't have to make any trips to the copy machine.

160 pages, softcover, $15.00

Journey Beyond Abuse
A Step-by-Step Guide to Facilitating Women's Domestic Abuse Groups

by Kay-Laurel Fischer, MA, LP, and Michael F. McGrane, LICSW

Create a program where women increase their understanding of the dynamics of abuse, feel less alone and isolated, feel empowered to make positive choices, and have a greater awareness of channels to safety. This book provides complete tools for facilitating effective groups. Includes twenty-one group activities which you can combine to create groups of differing length and focus. Also gives you tips on how to handle twenty-eight special issues such as child care, safety and protection, and substance abuse, plus much more.

208 pages, softcover, $45.00

Moving Beyond Abuse
(Companion guided journal to *Journey Beyond Abuse*)

A series of stories and questions that coordinate with the sessions provided in the facilitator's guide. The journal can be used in coordination with a women's group or with the guidance of a counselor in other forms of support for dealing with abuse issues. The open-ended questions provide gentle direction toward gaining insights that help affirm inner strength and heal the wounds of abuse.

88 pages, softcover, $10.00

What Works in Preventing Rural Violence

by Wilder Research Center

An in-depth review of eighty-eight effective strategies you can use to prevent and intervene in violent behavior, improve services for victims, and reduce repeat offenses. Strategies are organized into seven categories of violent acts—assaultive violence, child abuse, rape and sexual assault, domestic abuse, elder abuse, suicide, and bias (hate) crimes. Also includes a Community Report Card with step-by-step directions on how you can collect, record, and use information about violence in your community.

94 pages, softcover, $17.00

How to Order

 Call toll-free: **1-800-274-6024**
 8:00 am to 4:00 pm CST
(in Mpls./St. Paul: 651-659-6024)

 Fax order form to: **651-642-2061** (24 hours a day)

Mail order form to: A. H. Wilder Foundation
Publishing Center
919 Lafond Avenue
St. Paul, MN 55104

 E-mail your order to: **books@wilder.org**

Shipping

Standard Charges: *If order totals:* *Add:*

If order totals:	Add:
Up to $30.00	$4.00
$30.01 - 60.00	$5.00
$60.01 - 150.00	$6.00
$150.01 - 500.00	$8.00
Over $500.00	3% of order

- Orders are shipped UPS or Parcel Post. Please allow two weeks for delivery.
- For orders outside the U.S. or Canada, please add an additional U.S. $5.00
- Special RUSH delivery is available. Please call our toll-free phone number for rates.

Save money when you order in quantity

We offer substantial discounts on orders of ten or more copies of any single title. Please call for more information.

Send us your manuscript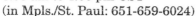

Wilder Publishing Center continually seeks manuscripts and proposals for publications in the fields of nonprofit management and community development. Send us your proposal or manuscript. Or, if you'd like more information, call us at 1-800-274-6024 and ask for our Author Guidelines or visit our Web site.

Visit our Web site at www.wilder.org

Order Form
Prices subject to change

	QTY.	PRICE EACH	TOTAL AMOUNT
Collaboration Handbook: Creating, Sustaining, and Enjoying the Journey		$28.00	
Collaboration: What Makes It Work		14.00	
Community Building: What Makes It Work		20.00	
Coping with Cutbacks: The Nonprofit Guide to Success When Times Are Tight		25.00	
Foundations for Violence-Free Living (facilitator's guide)		45.00	
On the Level (participant's workbook to Foundation's for Violence-Free Living)		15.00	
Journey Beyond Abuse (facilitator's guide)		45.00	
Moving Beyond Abuse (participant's journal)		10.00	
The Little Book of Peace (minimum order 10 copies)		0.65	
Marketing Workbook for Nonprofit Organizations Volume I		25.00	
Marketing Workbook for Nonprofit Organizations Volume II: Mobilize People for Marketing Success		25.00	
Pocket Guide for Marketing Representatives (one copy free with order of Marketing Volume II)		1.95	
Strategic Planning Workbook for Nonprofit Organizations, Revised and Updated		25.00	
What Works in Preventing Rural Violence		17.00	
		SUBTOTAL	
	In MN, please add 7% sales tax or attach exempt certificate		
		SHIPPING	
		TOTAL	

Amherst H. Wilder Foundation
Publishing Center
919 Lafond Avenue   **Toll-Free 1-800-274-6024**
St. Paul, MN 55104   Fax: (612) 642-2061

We occasionally make our mailing list available to carefully selected companies. If you do not wish to have your name included, please check here ☐

Name _____

Organization _____

Address _____

_____

City _____ State _____ ZIP _____

Phone *(in case we have questions)* (_____) _____

Payment Method VISA MasterCard AMERICAN EXPRESS Cards

Card # _____

Expiration Date _____

Signature (required) _____

☐ Check/Money Order (payable to A. H. Wilder Foundation)

☐ Bill Me (for orders under $100) Purchase Order # _____